Robert Jackson was born in Yorkshire in 1941 and was a fulltime author from 1969, specialising in aviation and military history. He speaks five different languages and has flown a variety of aircraft, and also lectures on pilot navigation and acts as a consultant to a helicopter company in North-East England.

ROBERT JACKSON

BOMBER!

CANELO HISTORY

First published in the United Kingdom in 1980 by Arthur Barker Limited

This edition published in the United Kingdom in 2023 by

Canelo
Unit 9, 5th Floor
Cargo Works, 1-2 Hatfields
London SE1 9PG
United Kingdom

A CIP catalogue record for this book is available from the British Library.

ISBN 9781804365328

Cover images © Richard Paver Photography. Used by permission.

Cover design by Dan Mogford

Look for more great books at www.canelo.co

Printed and bound in Great Britain by Clays Ltd, Elcograf S.p.A.

Chapter 1

North Sea Battle
September–December 1939

The pilot of the Dornier 18 flying-boat sighed and looked at the chronometer on his instrument panel. The hands pointed to 10:45 a.m. It was three hours since he had taken off from his base at Norderney; two hours of intense boredom, patrolling backwards and forwards along the Fisher Bank, with nothing in sight but the endless horizon. Below the Dornier, a solid, unbroken layer of cloud stretched as far as the eye could see, hiding the grey, choppy waters of the North Sea.

As he flew on, the Dornier pilot kept a watchful eye on the western sky. Just a couple of days earlier, a fellow pilot of 2/Aufklärungsgruppe (Reconnaissance Group) 106 had encountered a Lockheed Hudson patrol bomber of RAF Coastal Command over these waters, and had only just made it back to base with one engine out of action and a dying rear-gunner. The RAF seemed to be looking for trouble, and it paid to be careful.

It was 26 September 1939, and Britain had been at war with Germany for just over three weeks. So far, apart from a few skirmishes between British, French and German fighters over the Maginot Line, there had been little air activity on either side. Soon after the declaration of war on 3 September, the air-raid sirens had wailed over the streets of London and the British had believed that they were about to experience their first massive air attack, but it had never come. It had all been a false alarm. The following day, RAF bombers had made an abortive and costly daylight attack on German warships off Wilhelmshaven, but since then both sides had contented themselves with carrying out reconnaissance flights over the North Sea, probing each other's defences.

On this morning of 26 September the Dornier crews of 2/Aufklärungsgruppe 106 had been detailed to fly a reconnaissance mission on behalf of Navy Group West, who planned to send a force of destroyers out into the North Sea early the following morning. Because of the unbroken cloud cover, however, reconnaissance proved almost impossible, and the pilot of the Dornier over the Fisher Bank made up his mind to give it up as a bad job and return to base if there was not a marked improvement within the next half hour.

Suddenly, a shout from the observer rang in the pilot's headphones. He looked down. Miraculously, a gap had appeared in the clouds, revealing a patch of wrinkled grey sea. And there, right in the middle of the patch, was a ship. The pilot put the Dornier into a tight turn and kept his eyes glued on the break. Another ship came into view as he watched, followed by another and another. For an instant his mind refused to work, and then it dawned on him. He was looking at the British Home Fleet.

Hardly daring to believe his incredible good luck, the pilot radioed his report to Norderney. A few minutes after eleven o'clock, the telephone rang in the Luftwaffe operations room on the Frisian island of Sylt, headquarters of the medium bomber strike force of Fliegerkorps X.

'*Operational Orders. British battle squadron sighted in square Dora Bertholdt 4022. One aircraft carrier, four battleships, several cruisers and destroyers. Reconnaissance aircraft is maintaining contact with the enemy. All available aircraft are to take off and attack with 1,000-lb bombs.'*

The British naval force in fact consisted of the aircraft carrier *Ark Royal*, the battleships *Nelson* and *Rodney*, the battle cruisers *Hood* and *Renown* and three light cruisers. Not far away steamed the Second Cruiser Squadron, with four cruisers and a screen of six destroyers.

At 12:50, nine Heinkel He 111 bombers of Kampfgeschwader 26 – the 'Lion Wing' – took off from Westerland, led by Captain Vetter. They were followed a few minutes later by four Junkers 88 dive-bombers of Kampfgeschwader 30, the 'Eagle Wing', under Lieutenant Storp. It was the biggest force Fliegerkorps X could muster at such short notice, but this was the chance the pilots had been waiting for. After weeks of inactivity, here at last was a chance to come to grips with the British. Moreover, it was the Junkers 88's first operational sortie.

Hailed as a 'wonder bomber' by Hermann Göring, Commander-in-Chief of the Luftwaffe, the prototype Ju 88 had flown for the first time in December 1936, and at that time was faster than any fighter in widespread service with the world's air forces. The first batch of production Ju 88A-1s had been delivered to the Luftwaffe just after the outbreak of war. Powered by a pair of 1,200 hp Junkers Jumo 211B radial engines, the bomber had a top speed of 270 mph at 17,500 feet and carried a bomb load of 3,960 lbs. It was to become the most versatile and widely produced German bomber of the Second World War.

The four Junkers 88s of the 'Eagle Wing' slid low over the waves towards the north-west. At the controls of the third aircraft was Corporal Carl Francke; within twenty-four hours, his name would be splashed across the front page of every newspaper in Germany.

Francke had been one of the team of civilian test pilots who had flown the Ju 88 at Junkers' Rechlin factory before the war, and he knew the aircraft inside out. When war broke out he had volunteered for the Luftwaffe so that he could go on testing the bomber under operational conditions. Besides, he was not the kind of man who would be content to remain cooped up at Rechlin while there was a chance of seeing action in the air. His humble rank of corporal did not worry him in the least, for his status and experience made him a highly respected figure among KG 30's personnel.

Behind Francke, in the Ju 88's bulbous 'glasshouse' cockpit, sat the other three crew members: navigator, flight engineer and wireless operator/air gunner. They had been airborne for exactly two hours when they sighted the warships. Francke pulled back the stick and the Junkers shot up through the clouds, levelling out at 10,000 feet in brilliant sunshine.

Circling, he looked down through a broad rift in the cloud layer. There was the primary target: the rectangular shape of the aircraft carrier. He nosed the Junkers over into a dive, holding her steady as the carrier crept into his sights. There was no flak; the British could not have seen him yet.

Francke's hand tightened on the bomb release – and at that very moment a tuft of cloud drifted across the gap in front of him. By the time the Junkers had sped through it, the carrier was no longer in his sights. Cursing, he pulled the aircraft up to 10,000 feet again, pursued by wicked bursts of flak. The Tommies had woken up at last. For eight long minutes he circled, waiting for his opportunity. Then he dived again, streaking down through a veritable wall of anti-aircraft fire. This time he had a clear run and there was no mistake. The carrier grew bigger in his sights, his thumb jabbed down on the release and two 1,000-lb bombs dropped away from beneath the wings. Sweating, Francke pulled the Junkers out of its plummeting dive and raced for the safety of the clouds. Tufts of dirty brown flak swept past, unpleasantly close.

The excited voice of the rear-gunner burst over the intercom, reporting a near miss. Francke risked a glance back. A fountain of water was erupting hard by the carrier and cascading over the flight deck. A split second later, the pilot thought he saw a bright flash near the bow. Whether it was a hit, or the flash from a heavy anti-aircraft gun, he had no means of telling. But if it wasn't a hit, what had happened to the second bomb? No one had seen it explode in the water. In any event, there was no sense in lingering. The British warships were spreading a curtain of steel across the sky. Francke dived down until the Junkers was skimming just a few feet above the sea and headed flat out for home.

Back at Westerland, Francke's report created a sensation. He had attacked the carrier with two

1,000-lb bombs; he had observed a near miss twenty or thirty feet from the vessel and a possible hit near the bow. The commanding officer of KG 30, Colonel Siburg, was sceptical. If you hit a carrier with a thousand-pounder, he thought, you were bound to see some tangible result. But Francke had seen nothing – not even a burst of smoke. Meanwhile, at the headquarters of Fliegerkorps X, things were humming. The Senior Intelligence Officer, Major Harlinghausen, had sent out a reconnaissance aircraft to shadow the Home Fleet and find out exactly what had happened. At 3 p.m., the pilot reported that the enemy battle squadron, consisting of two battleships and a screen of light cruisers, was heading westward at high speed. There was no sign of the carrier. A little later, the pilot spotted a large patch of fuel oil. It was not particularly significant, because the North Sea was covered with similar patches. Nevertheless, Harlinghausen thought the information important enough to pass on to Berlin. There, the General Staff put two and two together – and made five. It was beginning to look, they thought optimistically, as though the *Ark Royal* and her sixty aircraft had gone to the bottom.

Göring, together with Luftwaffe chiefs Milch and Jeschonnek, advised caution before making a definite statement; they felt it was better to wait until the British made an announcement. However, the German propaganda machine had already got hold of the rumour. The Luftwaffe had sunk Britain's most modern aircraft carrier – with a single bomb! To Dr Goebbels, the German propaganda minister, it was like manna from heaven.

When Captain Helmuth Pohle, commander of KG 30's No. 1 Squadron, arrived in Westerland on the evening of 26 September, he found a harassed Francke waiting for him. The two men were old friends and their difference in rank did not come between them.

'For God's sake, Pohle,' said Francke, 'Can't we put a stop to all this damn nonsense? There isn't a word of truth in any of it!'

But there was nothing either of them could do. The German propagandists seemed to have been gripped by a kind of frenzy, and it was too late to stop them. The next day, in a report on the attack on the British warships, the official Wehrmacht war bulletin claimed that the *Ark Royal* had been sunk and several other ships damaged. The Luftwaffe had suffered no losses. Even Göring was going along with the farce now; he sent his personal good wishes to Francke, had him promoted lieutenant on the spot, and awarded him the Iron Cross First and Second Class, much to the pilot's embarrassment.

The British Admiralty countered with a dry announcement which stated that the *Ark Royal* had returned safely to base. The Germans labelled this as a trick on the part of the British to camouflage their 'heavy losses'. Then, at the beginning of October, came news which shattered the German myth once and for all. The *Ark Royal* was at sea again, taking part in the hunt for the German pocket battleship *Admiral Graf Spee* in the Atlantic. During the next two years she was to make her presence felt with a vengeance, her strike aircraft playing a notable part in the pursuit and destruction of the battleship *Bismarck*. It was not until 14 November 1941 that she was finally torpedoed and sunk in the Mediterranean by the submarine U–81.

On 9 October 1939 the Luftwaffe once again tried to strike a blow at British naval power when 127 Heinkel 111s and 21 Junkers 88s of KG 26 and KG 30 took off to search for the warships. It was to be a combined operation with the German

Navy; the battle cruiser *Gneisenau*, the cruiser *Köln* and nine destroyers had put to sea. The Luftwaffe, however, failed to find the target, and the aircraft returned to base with their bombs still on board after a long and fruitless search.

Then, on 16 October, two days after U-boat commander Gunther Prien had crept daringly into the big British naval base at Scapa Flow in the Orkneys in the U-47 and sunk the battleship *Royal Oak*, reconnaissance aircraft, which had been keeping a close watch on the east coast of Scotland, reported that the battle cruiser HMS *Hood* had entered the Firth of Forth and appeared to be making for the naval anchorage at Rosyth.

At 11 o'clock that morning, the Junkers 88s of No. 1 Squadron KG 30, took off from Westerland under the command of Helmuth Pohle with orders to attack the *Hood* and any other naval units they found at Rosyth. At last, six weeks after the outbreak of war, German bombers were to venture into British territory for the first time.

There were, however, certain conditions. On the personal orders of Adolf Hitler, the Ju 88 crews were not to attack the *Hood* if she had already entered harbour. Pohle was not surprised by the directive; at this stage of the war, both the Luftwaffe and the Royal Air Force had an unspoken, unwritten agreement that only enemy warships were to be attacked, and bombs were not to be dropped if there was a danger of causing civilian casualties.

Seventy-five minutes after take-off, Pohle's Ju 88s were roaring up the Firth of Forth. They were flying in loose battle formation; Intelligence had indicated that the RAF had only a handful of obsolescent Gloster Gladiator biplane fighters in Scotland. In fact, Intelligence was wrong. Fighter Command had two Spitfire squadrons, Nos 602 and 603, based at Turnhouse near Edinburgh, and that very morning the Hurricanes of No. 607 Squadron had flown into Drem on the southern bank of the Firth.

Pohle's formation droned on. From 13,000 feet, the crews could see the sprawling, smoke-shrouded complex of Edinburgh, then the spidery structure of the Forth Bridge, beneath their wings. And there, dead ahead on the north bank, was Rosyth.

The first ship that Pohle saw in the harbour was the *Hood*, dwarfing the lesser warships that clustered around her. She presented a beautiful target. Pohle ground his teeth, remembering Hitler's order, but there were several other cruisers and destroyers anchored in the Firth and he selected a target, pushing the Junkers over into a dive. The flak was coming up in streams, exploding with a horrible gritty crunch, rocking the aircraft with near misses. Pohle fought to hold the Junkers steady as it screamed downhill in an 80-degree dive.

Suddenly, there was a loud bang and a gale of cold air roared into the cockpit. Pohle glanced up: the transparent escape hatch in the cockpit roof had gone. Desperately, he forced his attention back to the target, which now filled his sights. A second later, his two thousand pounders fell away and he was rocketing skywards again, crushed down into his seat by the 'g'. One of the bombs exploded in the water; the other hit the cruiser HMS *Southampton* starboard amidships, smashed through three decks, emerged from the side of the hull and reduced the Admiral's barge to matchwood. It failed to explode.

The rear-gunner's voice came over the intercom, warning that enemy fighters were coming in astern. They were the Spitfires of 603 Squadron. The rear-gunner watched as the first of them bored in, holding his fire until the last possible moment.

The leading Spitfire was flown by Squadron Leader E. E. Stevens. Smoky lines of tracer from the Junkers' rear gun flickered past his wings. He jabbed his thumb down on the firing-button and saw strikes sparkling and dancing on the 88's dark green camouflage. There was a flicker of fire from one engine and the Junkers started to go down, two more Spitfires attacking it in turn. It was the first time the nimble little fighters had fired their guns in anger.

Pohle's cockpit was a shambles. Both engineer and rear-gunner were dead, and the navigator was lying on the cockpit floor in a pool of blood, a bullet through his lungs. Pohle spotted a trawler and turned towards it, using all his strength to keep the aircraft flying on one engine. Then the Junkers ploughed into the sea with a jarring crash and he lost consciousness. A few minutes later the trawler crew fished him out of the sinking aircraft and he woke up five days later in Port Edwards hospital. His war was over.

Besides Pohle, KG 30 lost one other crew during this raid. The Ju 88s had inflicted only light damage on the cruisers *Southampton* and *Edinburgh* and the destroyer *Mohawk*. The next morning KG 30's No. 1 Squadron was in action again, under a new commanding officer; this time the target was the naval base at Scapa Flow. But apart from the old depot ship *Iron Duke*, which was damaged by a near miss, they found the nest empty. The Home Fleet had sought refuge in the Clyde on the west coast of Scotland, out of range of the bombers.

The Luftwaffe had failed to score a victory over the Royal Navy. Before the year was out, however, there was to be a victory of a different kind reaped by the German fighters; a victory that was to have no small effect on the RAF's bombing policies for a long time to come.

On 3 December, twenty-four Wellington bombers of Nos 38, 115 and 149 Squadrons took off from their bases at Marham and Mildenhall to attack enemy warships in the Heligoland Bight. Led by Wing Commander R. Kellet, the bombers made rendezvous over Great Yarmouth at 9:40 a.m., climbing to 10,000 feet over the sea en route to their objective. The leading flight of three aircraft sighted Heligoland at 11:26 and the crews made out the outlines of some ships, including two cruisers, lying in the vicinity.

The Wellingtons ran through heavy anti-aircraft fire as they made their approach and two of them were hit, although not seriously. A few moments later the bombers were attacked from astern by Messerschmitt 109s and 110s. These attacks were ineffective and at least one of the fighters was damaged. The Wellingtons bombed from 8,000 feet, but although some of their bombs fell in the target area no hits were registered on the warships. All the aircraft returned to base.

This operation seemed to justify the belief that a tight bomber formation was sufficient defence against fighter attacks in daylight. The Messerschmitt pilots had seemed wary of facing the Wellingtons' rear armament at a range closer than 400 yards, and although one straggling bomber had been attacked simultaneously by four fighters it had fought its way clear without having sustained a single hit.

Designed by Dr Barnes Wallis, who was later to conceive the special mines used to breach the Mohne and Eder dams during the famous RAF raid of May 1943, the Vickers Wellington was one of the war's outstanding aircraft. In 1939, when 179 were in service with the RAF, it was certainly the best machine available to Bomber Command. Powered by two 1,000 hp Bristol Pegasus radial engines it could carry a bomb load of 4,000 lbs, and later versions could lift 6,000. It had a six-man crew, and defensive armament was six .303 Browning machine-guns. In designing the Wellington, Wallis had employed geodetic construction, a method in which comparatively light strips of metal formed a web-like structure in both wings and fuselage. Apart from being light it was extremely rugged, and Wellingtons were capable of sustaining appalling battle damage and still remaining in the air.

Bomber Command was sufficiently encouraged by the result of the 3 December raid to try again. The opportunity came on the fourteenth, when it was reported that the cruisers *Nürnberg* and *Leipzig* had been torpedoed by a British submarine and were limping back to the Jade Estuary, badly damaged. At 11:45 a.m., twelve Wellingtons of No. 99 Squadron, led by Wing Commander J. F. Griffiths, took off from Newmarket to attack the warships. The weather was bad, with 10/10ths cloud at less than 1,000 feet, and by the time the

Dutch coast was sighted at 1:05 p.m. the Wellingtons were forced to fly at six hundred feet or less in order to say below the overcast. The pilots had been ordered not to attack unless they could bomb from at least 2,000 feet; they nevertheless continued on course in the hope that the cloud would lift.

By this time they were coming under heavy and continuous fire from warships and armed merchantmen lying in the approaches to the estuary. At this low altitude the bombers presented excellent targets and several were hit. Suddenly, there was a lull in the flak as enemy fighters came speeding up; they were the Messerschmitt 109s of II/JG 77, led by Major Harry von Bülow, and this time the pilots showed no hesitation in pressing home their attacks to point-blank range. The Wellingtons' gunners accounted for one Bf 109, which was seen to crash in flames, but the fighters destroyed five bombers in a matter of minutes. A sixth Wellington crashed on landing at Newmarket.

Despite the unfortunate outcome of this raid, another attack on the German fleet was planned for 18 December. Twenty-four Wellingtons of Nos 9, 37 and 149 Squadrons under the leadership of

Wing Commander Kellet assembled over King's Lynn shortly after 9 a.m. The aircraft were loaded with 500-lb semi-armour-piercing bombs and the crews' orders were to attack any shipping located in the Schillig Roads, Wilhelmshaven or the Jade Estuary. Any bombing was to be carried out from at least 10,000 feet.

The bombers climbed to 14,000 feet in four flights of six aircraft. Less than an hour after leaving the English coast they were flying in a cloudless sky, with visibility more than thirty miles. About two-thirds of the way across, two aircraft dropped out with engine trouble and returned to base.

At 10:50 the bombers were detected by two experimental radar stations on Heligoland and Wangerooge, both equipped with the new 'Freya' detection apparatus. The officer in charge of the station on Wangerooge immediately alerted the fighter operations room at Jever, only to be told by the duty officer that something must be wrong with his radar set; the British would never be fool-hardy enough to mount an attack in a cloudless sky and brilliant sunshine, where their aircraft would be sitting targets for the German fighters.

Meanwhile, the twenty-two Wellingtons had made a detour round Heligoland to avoid the anti-aircraft batteries there and were now turning in towards Wilhemshaven from the south. After a delay of several minutes the first German fighters, six Messerschmitt 109s of 10/JG 26, led by First Lieutenant Johannes Steinhoff, took off from Jever to intercept. None of the other fighter units at Jever or the adjacent airfield of Wangerooge was on readiness, and there was a further delay before these were 'scrambled'.

Steinhoff's 109s met the Wellingtons on the approach to Wilhelmshaven and scored their first two kills almost immediately. The fighters then sheered off as the bombers flew at 13,000 feet through heavy flak over the naval base. The Wellingtons crossed Wilhelmshaven without dropping any bombs, then turned and crossed it again, still without bombing, before heading away towards the north-west. By this time, the Bf 109s of 10/JG 26 had been joined by the twin-engined Messerschmitt 110s of ZG 76 and the 109s of JG 77, and the combined force of fighters now fell on the Wellington formation as it passed to the north of Wangerooge.

Another bomber went down, the victim of a Bf 110, and crash-landed on the island of Borkum. Only one member of the crew survived. Other Bf 110s accounted for five more Wellingtons in an area some fifteen miles north-west of Borkum, and a sixth bomber was destroyed thirty miles north of the Dutch island of Ameland. Rather belatedly, a pair of 109s from JG 101 at Neumünster arrived and joined the air battle in time to catch the tail-end of the Wellington formation; they shot down one bomber, but one of the Messerschmitts was badly hit and the pilot had to make a forced landing.

In one home-bound Wellington, the pilot, Sergeant J. Ramshaw, found himself suddenly sitting in an icy gale as a 110's cannon shells blasted away the nose of the aircraft. The bomber was in a pitiful state; the fabric of the wings was torn and flapping in the slipstream, the metal of the engine nacelles was torn to shreds by jagged splinters. The rear-gunner, Leading Aircraftman Lilley, was killed outright and the front-gunner, Aircraftman Driver, had his turret wrecked and the barrels of his guns shot clean away. With petrol streaming by the gallon from holed fuel tanks, Sergeant Ramshaw was forced to ditch the bomber in the sea. Luckily, the survivors were picked up by a British trawler and they were put ashore safely at Grimsby the following morning. Two more Wellingtons also ditched in similar circumstances.

The raid, from which twelve bombers had failed to return, caused severe repercussions throughout RAF Bomber Command. One shortcoming in particular had contributed to the disaster: the fuel tank in the Wellington's port wing was neither self-sealing nor protected by armour plate, and when hit in this area the bombers had caught fire very rapidly. Those which did not burn lost vast quantities of fuel through holes punched in these vulnerable tanks. Within days of the raid, a priority programme was initiated to fit extra armour plate to the fuel tanks of all Bomber Command aircraft.

Most important of all, the appalling losses suffered by the Wellingtons highlighted the folly of sending bombers deep into enemy territory in broad daylight without fighter escort. After December 1939, RAF Bomber Command's policy was to operate increasingly under cover of darkness, while later in the war the Americans were to adhere to the theory that bomber formations with heavy defensive armament were capable of making successful daylight penetration attacks.

The Americans, too, were destined to learn the hard way.

Chapter 2

Ordeal of a City
Rotterdam, May 1940

The aircraft droned in from the sea, across the long sweep of coastline that ended in the Hook of Holland. To the left lay the Hague, while over on the right, half hidden in the morning mist, was the cluster of broad, low-lying islands that marked the place where the River Schelde spilled its waters into the North Sea.

The aircraft were twin-engined Heinkel III bombers. There were twenty-eight of them, and they belonged to No. 2 Squadron, Kampfgeschwader 4. They had taken off from their base at Delmenhorst shortly before 5 a.m., and now, ninety minutes later, they were almost within sight of their target: the airport of Waalhaven, on the outskirts of Rotterdam.

In an attempt to confuse the Dutch defences, 2/KG 4's commander, Colonel Martin Fiebig, had led his squadron in a wide detour around northern Holland, approaching Rotterdam from the west. As the bombers swept over the coast, however, their pilots finding it difficult to see because of the blinding sun, a curtain of flak rose to meet them. It seemed that the Dutch were wide awake after all.

A few minutes later, the Heinkels were attacked by half a dozen nimble little Fokker D.21 fighters of the 2nd Air Regiment, Netherlands Army Air Force. One of them fastened itself to Fiebig's tail and raked the bomber from wingtip to wingtip. With both engines in flames, the Heinkel skidded and began to lose height, its crew baling out. The rest of the bombers droned on towards Waalhaven. In Rotterdam, the air-raid sirens were howling full blast. Simultaneously, other Luftwaffe bomber formations were bearing down on the airfields of Amsterdam-Schipol, Ypenburg and Bergen op Zoom, with the object of paralysing Holland's small airforce with one blow.

The Heinkels of 2/KG 4, their formation still virtually intact, swept over Waalhaven and unloaded their bombs with deadly precision. Hundreds of Dutch troops were killed when the hangar in which they were billeted, straddled by a stick of bombs, collapsed on top of them and caught fire. Thunderous detonations crashed out through the pall of smoke which rose high in the still air above the airfield. A few seconds later, a second formation of aircraft came drumming purposefully towards Waalhaven, out of the sunrise this time. They were Junkers 52 transports, and as they circled the airfield sticks of paratroops fell from their bellies. Within five minutes the sky was filled with billowing canopies as the airborne troops drifted down in a great ring around Waalhaven. One Junkers, hit by flak, swerved off course just as the paratroops spilled from it. Many of them plunged helplessly to their deaths among the burning hangars.

The paratroops landed around the airfield perimeter and relentlessly began to close in on the airfield defences. In the general confusion, six more Junkers 52s swept down to land on the airfield. Before they had rolled to a stop, more troops poured from them and attacked the Dutch defenders from the rear. Within a quarter of an hour it was all over. Hopelessly outnumbered, the Dutch were overwhelmed and the last isolated pockets of resistance mopped up.

It was not yet eight o'clock. The date was 10 May 1940, and Holland was receiving her baptism of fire. The long months of the 'phoney war' were over, and everywhere – in Belgium, Holland, and northern France – the Luftwaffe's bombers were striking at airfields and communications, paving the way for the armoured divisions of the Wehrmacht which were rolling westwards through the forests of the Ardennes and across the River Meuse.

Holland was a vital factor in the overall German invasion strategy. To make the invasion's northern flank secure, Holland had to be overrun as quickly as possible, which was why the Germans had decided to seize key objectives with the use of airborne forces. Waalhaven was in German hands, but the most important objectives still remained to be captured: the bridges over the Maas in the centre of Rotterdam. These bridges, together with others at Dordrecht and Moerdijk, were the only three major crossing-points over the great natural anti-tank barrier formed by the wide estuaries of the Maas and the Rhine. The German airborne troops were given the task of capturing them and holding them until the tanks of the 9th Panzer Division fought their way through, opening the road into the heart of Holland.

The bridges at Moerdijk and Dordrecht were captured early on 10 May by paratroops of General Kurt Student's 7th Airborne Division, who managed to retain their foothold despite determined Dutch counter-attacks. In both cases the paratroops were air-dropped nearby, but in Rotterdam the technique was different. At 7 a.m., while the Germans were consolidating their position in Waalhaven, twelve Heinkel He 59 floatplanes landed on the Nieuwe Maas and disgorged a total of 120 paratroops, who paddled ashore in rubber rafts. Within a few minutes, they had succeeded in establishing a foothold on both banks of the Maas, at either end of the big Willems bridge and the adjacent railway bridge. They quickly set up their machine-guns, surrounded themselves with belts and clips of ammunition and prepared themselves for a bitter fight: a fight that was to last five days and four nights while a paratroop battalion from Waalhaven tried in vain to battle its way through the streets of Rotterdam to get to them.

The Dutch made several attempts to bomb the bridges. On the morning of 11 May two of the Dutch Air Arm's nine Fokker T.V medium bombers tried to break through to the centre of Rotterdam. It was hopeless. They were immediately pounced on by patrolling Messerschmitts; one was shot down and the other was damaged so badly that it could no longer be made airworthy. Two days later, another Fokker – the only surviving Dutch bomber by this time – attacked the bridge at Moerdijk and was shot to pieces by 20-mm flak.

Elsewhere, things were going badly for the German airborne troops. At Ypenburg, north of Delft, eleven out of thirteen Junkers 52s in the first wave had been destroyed by flak and obstacles on the airfield itself. Thick columns of smoke rose skywards from the burning wrecks. Survivors staggered from the crumpled fuselages and were immediately mown down by Dutch machine-gun fire.

Many Junkers landed on the beach north of the Hague. With supreme courage, Dutch airmen flying antiquated Fokker C.5 and C.10 biplanes crept in beneath the umbrella of Messerschmitts and strafed the masses of men and equipment on the beaches. By nightfall, the German forces in the Hague area had been virtually annihilated. The beaches were littered with the carcases of Ju 52s which had become bogged down in the clinging sand. Lieutenant-General Graf Sponeck, whose pilot had brought down his Junkers in the middle of a ploughed field, desperately tried to rally the scattered German forces. Just before dusk on 10 May Sponeck managed to establish radio contact with Kesselring, chief of Luftflotte 2. Kesselring ordered Sponeck to forget about an assault on the Hague – seat of the Dutch Government and Royal Family – and instead to fight his way through to Rotterdam. Sponeck heard his orders with misgivings. He was a man of no illusions. It was all his men could do to hold on to their precarious foothold on the coast, let alone march on Rotterdam. Things were beginning to look black.

They were still looking black thirty-six hours later when Major-General Hubicki's 9th Panzer Division finally rolled over the Moerdijk bridge on the morning of 13 May, cheered by its haggard defenders. The Panzers raced on through Dordrecht, and that evening they clattered into the outskirts of Rotterdam south of the Maas. Among the shattered houses near the southern end of the Willens Bridge they ground to a halt, pinned down by heavy artillery fire. The paratroops were still clinging bitterly to their tenuous foothold on the northern end of the bridge. Their losses had been heavy, and the survivors were exhausted. They had been in action continually for nearly four days. There was no question of withdrawal across the bullet-swept bridge.

Command of the German forces in Rotterdam now rested on the shoulders of Rudolf Schmidt, general of the 39th Panzer Korps. He had been ordered at all costs to avoid unnecessary casualties among the Dutch civilians. On the evening of 13 May Schmidt called upon the Dutch commander, Colonel Scharroo, to surrender, stating that further resistance would lead to widespread damage in the city and would only delay the inevitable capitulation by a few more hours.

But every one of those hours would mean a serious loss of time to the Germans. General von Küchler, C.-in-C. of the 18th Army, feared that a British landing in Holland was imminent. The Dutch had to be broken quickly; the German forces already committed against them were desperately needed for the push through Belgium into Northern France.

At 7 p.m., von Küchler ordered that the Dutch resistance in Rotterdam was to be smashed by every available means. The battle-plan envisaged a tank attack across the Willems Bridge at 3:30 the following afternoon, preceded by a large-scale air raid on the surrounding area to 'soften up' the Dutch.

By the morning of the fourteenth the Dutch commander still had not replied to General Schmidt's call for surrender. Two German envoys had been flown into the city to discuss capitulation terms. Finally, at noon, they managed to get in touch with Colonel Scharroo and delivered their ultimatum: surrender, or suffer the destruction of the city centre by the Luftwaffe. Scharroo found himself unable to make the decision alone. He told the envoys that he would have to get in touch with the Hague for further instructions. Half an hour later, the Dutch Government replied that it was sending a delegation to Rotterdam to talk terms with the Germans. The deputation was due to arrive at 2 p.m.

At 1:30 General Schmidt sent a signal to Luftflotte 2, calling off the impending air attack, which was scheduled for 3 p.m. It was too late. Rotterdam was already doomed.

At 1:25, the last of one hundred Heinkel 111s of Kampfgeschwader 54 had taken off from their airfields near Bremen. By the time Schmidt's signal reached Luftflotte 2, the Heinkels were already approaching the Dutch border. And by the time KG 54's headquarters received the order to scrub the mission, the bombers were already inside Dutch territory. This meant that the radio operator in each aircraft had now closed down his position to take up his combat station behind the machine-gun in the blister beneath the fuselage. Frantically, KG 54's controllers tried to establish radio contact with the bombers. In vain.

There was now only one slender hope: that the German troops in Rotterdam would be able to fire two flares, the abort signal, in time to stop the attack.

The He 111s thundered towards Rotterdam in two waves. One, led by Colonel Lackner, KG 54's commander, approached from the east; the other, headed by Lieutenant-Colonel Hohne – commander of No. 1 Squadron, KG 54 – made a wide detour to attack from the south-west.

Strapped to his knee each bomber pilot had a map of the city, with the Dutch-held zones at either end of the bridges outlined in red. It was precisely within these sectors that the pilots had to place their bombs.

Five minutes past three. Lackner's bombers roared in over the outskirts of the city from the south. Clusters of dirty black shell-bursts from the Dutch flak batteries blossomed out around the formation. Lackner screwed up his eyes and peered ahead, searching for the target along the line of the river, which curved through Rotterdam in a sharp loop. It was hard to see anything at all; the city was shrouded by a veil of dusty haze and smoke, through which the sun, away to the left, glared with a piercing radiance. It was hardly surprising that the pilots never saw the red flares which the German ground forces were shooting off in desperation...

The Heinkels droned over the island in the middle of the Maas and unloaded their 250- and 500-lb bombs smack in the centre of the Old Town, where the Dutch artillery was in position. Like great black birds silhouetted against the brassy sky, the bombers wheeled to the right and vanished in the haze. A few seconds later, Hohne's formation came roaring in from the south-west.

In the cockpit of his Heinkel, Hohne concentrated on following the instructions of his bombardier as the latter guided him on to the target, where fires could be seen blazing fiercely amid piles of rubble.

Just as the bombardier pressed the release and the Heinkel leaped buoyantly as its load dropped away, Hohne caught an elusive glimpse of a flicker of light above the Maas island. There it was again – no doubt about it this time. A red flare! He turned to his wireless operator and yelled 'Abort!' Feverishly, the operator passed on the message to the other bombers. No one else had seen the red flare. Puzzled, the other pilots followed Hohne through a 180-degree turn and left the city behind, their bombs still on board.

Fifty-seven out of the hundred Heinkels of KG 54 – those of the first wave and Hohne's own aircraft – had dropped a hundred tons of bombs on Rotterdam, pulverizing the city centre. Fire swept through the shattered streets, consuming everything in its path. A great pillar of smoke rose into the still afternoon air, darkening the sun. Beneath the debris lay the bodies of over nine hundred Dutch civilians.

At 5 p.m., just two hours after the attack, the Dutch garrison in Rotterdam surrendered. At 7 p.m., the Panzers rolled across the Maas bridges towards the north. The airborne troops, who had held the bridges for so long, stood in silence as the monsters clattered by, too exhausted even to raise a cheer.

First reports of the attack on Rotterdam reached the British War Cabinet in London the following morning. They indicated, quite erroneously, that thousands of innocent people lay dead beneath the rubble of the city centre; in fact, a figure of 30,000 killed was accepted in many quarters for years after the war.

The raid on Rotterdam had, in the event, turned out to be a tragic blunder, but this did not alter the fact that the Germans had conceived and executed it as a deliberate terror attack against a civilian target, despite the presence of Dutch Army units in the area. The grim conclusion drawn by the War Cabinet was that the enemy had taken off the gloves, and that the 'gentlemen's agreement' of the early months of the war, restricting bombing on humanitarian grounds to targets where there was little chance of civilian lives being lost, was at an end. In fact, the 'agreement' had never been anything other than tenuous; the campaign in Poland, in September 1939, had clearly shown that German blitzkrieg tactics did not exclude devastating air attacks on densely populated towns and cities under the pretext of hastening the end of enemy resistance. Warsaw, however, had been a long way from London, and of little more significance than a name on the map to most Britons; Rotterdam, on the other hand, was practically on the doorstep, and the destruction of a large part of this ancient city cried out for retaliation.

Nevertheless, despite the severe jolt administered to British strategic bombing policy by the Rotterdam raid, it was only after much discussion – and with great reluctance – that RAF Bomber Command was finally authorized to attack targets east of the Rhine on 15 May. That night, a force of ninety-nine Wellingtons, Whitleys and Hampdens was despatched to attack oil plants, steelworks and railway targets in the Ruhr valley. Only a small portion of the total force sent out located the industrial targets, but considerable damage was inflicted on a number of railway junctions and marshalling yards in this first attack by the RAF on Germany's industrial heartland.

Up to 15 June, the RAF's heavy bombers carried out twenty-seven night attacks on targets inside German territory. These early raids were haphazard, with little attempt at co-ordination between individual crews, let alone squadrons. It was left to each crew to fix their own take-off time, route to the target and bombing attitude. The damage they caused was insignificant, and their efforts failed to disrupt even a fraction of the enemy's invasion timetable. Yet, in a sense, they were pioneers, blazing a path across darkened Europe for the mighty bomber streams which, within three years, would subject Germany's cities to an ordeal that would render Rotterdam's agony tiny by comparison.

Chapter 3

First Bombs on Berlin

When the Germans attacked on the western front on 10 May 1940, the French Air Force possessed a total of four hundred bombers – on paper. In fact, only 184 were fully serviceable and ready for combat operations, and a high proportion of these were obsolete models which stood little chance of survival in a hostile environment where Messerschmitts ruled the sky.

The most modern bomber in French service was the Liore et Olivier LeO 451, a graceful, streamlined machine powered by two Gnome-Rhone radial engines which gave it a top speed of over 280 mph at 13,000 feet – faster than the German Junkers 88. In May 1940 110 LeOs were on the French Air Force's inventory, but only fifty-nine were actually in service with operational units; the remainder were still at the factory, awaiting delivery. Conversion to the new type had proved a slow and tricky process for crews used to fixed-undercarriage bombers with half the LeO's speed, and fifteen of the new aircraft had been destroyed in training accidents between September 1939 and May 1940. The LeO 451, which had a crew of four, carried a defensive armament of one 20-mm cannon and two 7.5-mm machine-guns. Its maximum bomb load was 2,800 lbs.

In the north-east zone of operations, which bore the brunt of the enemy assault, the mainstay of the French bomber force was the elderly Amiot 143M, a twin-engined type with a fixed under-carriage. Completely outdated, it lumbered along at a speed of 150 mph. It carried a crew of five, a defensive armament of four 7.5-mm machine-guns and a 2,000-lb bomb load.

During the first three days of the German offensive the Amiot-equipped squadrons carried out intensive night operations against enemy troop and vehicle concentrations in the Ardennes region. By the end of the three-day period of maximum effort the crews and their aircraft were exhausted. The four squadrons involved had a total of only twenty-one serviceable aircraft out of forty-five, and yet the greatest sacrifices were still to come.

On 14 May eighteen Amiots were ordered to stand by for a low-level daylight attack against enemy columns in the Sedan sector, where the Germans were breaking through in strength. Flown by volunteer crews, they took off from their bases at 11:25 a.m., each aircraft carrying sixteen 100-lb and two 220-lb bombs. Half an hour after take-off six of the Amiots turned back, having failed to make rendezvous with their fighter escort. The remainder pressed on towards their targets in the Sedan-Givonne-Bazeille sector.

At 12:15 the formation passed to the south of Mezieres, flying at 1,000 feet under cloud cover. A few minutes later the bombers were over the broad ribbon of the Meuse, and a gentle turn brought them in towards Sedan from the north. So far, it was like a peacetime training flight; the sky was completely empty.

Suddenly, the sky was filled with flak bursts and glowing trails of 20-mm shells. An Amiot was hit and began to drag a long ribbon of flame, plunging earthwards like a torch. Three of the crew baled out and were taken prisoner. At that moment six more Amiots broke formation and turned towards the Meuse bridges, presenting their fighter escort with a problem. The fighters – Morane 406s – now had to cover two attacking forces. The six Amiots that adhered to their original target continued their run-in and unloaded their bombs on the congested roads north of Sedan, lurching as flak hit them again and again. One machine broke formation, trailing smoke, and began a descending turn towards friendly territory. Despite being attacked by an enemy fighter the pilot, Lieutenant Foucher, managed to regain his base after flying the whole way at tree-top height.

As the bombers roared out of the flak zone, throttles wide open, the Messerschmitts pounced. A pair of Messerschmitt 110s fastened themselves on to the tails of two Amiots, one of which was quickly shot down. The crew baled out. The other aircraft received three 20-mm shells in its port engine, which began to stream dense white smoke; a fourth shell shattered the port undercarriage, a fifth ripped the pilot's parachute pack to shreds and a sixth tore away the co-pilot's control column. The pilot, Adjudant Milan, made his escape into a bank of cumulus cloud and crash-landed in a field a few minutes later. The crew got out safely, but the aircraft was a complete wreck.

By some miracle, all the other Amiots in the Sedan operation returned to base, although all of them were shot to ribbons and not one was in a battleworthy condition. A simultaneous attack had been made in the same area by eight unescorted LeO 451s; one received a direct flak hit in the bomb bay and exploded in mid-air. The other seven got away, but in this case too, battle damage rendered them all unserviceable. The small RAF bomber force in France – consisting of single-engined Fairey Battle light bombers and twin-engined Bristol Blenheims – suffered even more tragically in operations that day against the Sedan bridgeheads; losses amounted to forty aircraft, or sixty-five per cent of the total force committed.

The disaster of 14 May marked the virtual end of the Anglo-French tactical bombing effort against the German armoured spearheads. It would be more than two weeks before the Allied bomber squadrons were able to resume operations in comparative strength, and by that time the Battle of France would already have been lost, with the British Expeditionary Force and part of the French army in the north in the throes of evacuation from Dunkirk and the Germans preparing to swing southwards for the final offensive along the line of the River Somme.

Yet, amid all the chaos and misery of almost continual retreat, there shone deeds of courage and dedication that were to be an inspiration to those who followed in later years, as individual Frenchmen fought their own battle against the floodtide that burst across their land for the second time in a quarter of a century. One such was Commandant Dailliere, the central figure in one of the most astonishing air dramas to emerge from World War II.

In October 1939, a month after the outbreak of war, several French naval officers were summoned urgently to Paris to be briefed for a 'special mission'. The officers had only been in uniform for a few weeks, having been called up with France's reserve forces when hostilities with Germany seemed inevitable. All had one thing in common; in peacetime, they had formed the crews of the giant Farman and Latecoere transport aircraft which plied the intercontinental air routes between France and her colonies.

In Paris, the officers learned that the French Admiralty had requisitioned a pair of Farman 222/3 transports belonging to Air France, and that they were to fly these machines on long-range maritime patrol duties over the South Atlantic. Their primary mission was to locate and track the German pocket battleships *Admiral Graf Spee* and *Admiral Scheer*, which were threatening the Allied trade routes. For this purpose, the aircraft were to be based in Brazil.

The two machines took off from Bordeaux on 8 October 1939 and headed south, Bordeaux being the only field with a long enough strip − 1,200 metres − to allow them to get airborne with a full load of fuel. After a non-stop flight of over sixteen hours they reached Dakar in East Africa, where they refuelled in readiness for the next leg: the $14\frac{1}{2}$-hour transatlantic crossing. Arriving in Brazil late on the eleventh they started their operational task almost at once, ranging far out over the ocean in search of the elusive warships. Since Brazil was neutral, the aircraft − which were still in Air France livery − carried out their reconnaissance flights under the guise of weather research. Their efforts, however, drew a complete blank, and they were recalled to France in November. One of them, the

Laurent-Guerrero, skidded off the runway on take-off at Dakar and was completely wrecked, although the crew escaped unhurt.

Meanwhile, the French Admiralty had requisitioned three more Air France transports; new Farman 223/4s, all factory fresh and all named after celebrated French scientific writers of the nineteenth century – *Jules Verne*, *Camille Flammarion* and *Leverrier*. They were militarized by the addition of machine-guns, and in theory at least they could each carry three tons of bombs over a range of 3,000 miles. The three aircraft were placed under the command of Commandant Dailliere, an experienced long-range pilot who had led the transatlantic detachment, and various schemes were put forward for their use during the winter of 1939–40. One such was to employ them in laying magnetic mines in the Gulf of Bothnia, between Finland and Sweden, through which a high proportion of Germany's vital iron-ore traffic passed. In the event this scheme came to nothing, although the *Jules Verne* was modified to carry bombs or mines on external racks under the wings – the interior of the fuselage being almost entirely taken up by auxiliary fuel tanks, with only a narrow catwalk from nose to tail. Neither of the other two machines was modified in this way, and work only began on them after the German invasion of France in May 1940. It was never completed, and *Jules Verne* consequently became the only Farman 223 to carry out offensive operations.

During the period of the 'phoney war', early in 1940, Dailliere had strongly advocated using the *Jules Verne* to bomb targets in Germany, Berlin being at the top of his list. The French Admiralty, however, refused to agree to such a plan, not only because the bombing of enemy territory was not yet Allied policy at this stage of the war, but because Dailliere, with his vast experience, was considered too valuable a person to risk his life on a mission of this kind.

Nevertheless, Dailliere and his crew carried out many practice bombing missions in the spring of 1940, and on 11 May – the day after the start of the German offensive in the west – they were briefed to carry out their first offensive sortie. At dusk, the *Jules Verne* took off from its base at Lanveoc-Poulmic, on the Cherbourg peninsula, and flew to Aachen, where it dropped a few bombs in the vicinity of the railway station. On the way home it bombed the bridges at Maastricht, over which the German armoured divisions were pouring into the Low Countries. The damage caused in both attacks was negligible. The next mission, on the night of 13/14 May, was against road junctions on the island of Walcheren, where units of the French Seventh Army – which had advanced deep into Holland – were cut off and isolated.

The third and fourth missions, on 16 and 20 May, were once again flown against rail targets in Aachen. The second of these sorties was particularly exacting for the crew, for the night was brilliantly clear and the German defences were fully on the alert. The *Jules Verne* was flying at only 1,200 feet, following the main railway line that led towards the objective, Aachen station, when suddenly the aircraft was caught in a web of dozens of search-lights. The big machine was still uncamouflaged and her silver paintwork glittered in the intense light, making her a sitting target.

Although Dailliere was aircraft captain, the *Jules Verne* was flown on this occasion by Master Pilot Queugnet, who now took her down to rooftop level and began a series of violent evasive manoeuvres. Dailliere, half-blinded by the searchlights, ordered the pilot to make two runs over the station before releasing his bombs. Although the flak was intense, the big aircraft miraculously collected only two small splinter holes before making its escape – the only battle damage it was to suffer throughout its extraordinary career. There was, however, one casualty as a result of this attack: Master pilot Queugnet, who was so physically exhausted by the strain of throwing the huge, ponderous machine around the sky at low level that he had to be replaced by Master Pilot Yonnet, who piloted the *Jules Verne* on all her subsequent missions.

During the closing days of May the *Jules Verne* undertook several tactical operations, notably against German armoured concentrations in the Clair Marais Forest and an important railway junction near Saint-Omer. Dailliere, meanwhile, had been continuing to seek approval for a raid on Berlin, but at the end of May – even with the French armies collapsing on all sides – the Government was still reluctant to approve such a step for fear of reprisals. It was only on 4 June, following a large-scale attack by the Luftwaffe on targets in the Paris area, that the French authorities relented and Dailliere was ordered to put his plans into action.

The French Admiralty, which had been the sole authority governing the *Jules Verne*'s operations so far, already possessed a considerable dossier of target photographs and maps of the Berlin area, which Dailliere and his crew had memorized by heart. By this time the *Jules Verne* and her two sister Farmans had been formed into an official French Navy unit, Escadrille B5, which was based at Bordeaux-Merignac on the coast, and to achieve maximum surprise Dailliere decided to route the flight to Berlin over water for as long as possible, the aircraft flying over the Channel and the North Sea before turning eastwards across the 'neck' of Denmark, north of Kiel, and approaching the German capital from the north. The attack was to be made from a height of not less than 4,500 feet because of the danger from barrage balloons, and under no circumstances were bombs to be dropped on densely-populated areas. The whole mission, in fact, was to be of little more than psychological value.

The *Jules Verne* took off from Merignac on the long outward journey at three o'clock in the afternoon of 7 June, the flight timed so that the aircraft would arrive over Denmark just as darkness was falling. As it lumbered along the Channel coast at 160 mph, labouring under the weight of fuel and bombs it carried, it was fired on several times by the trigger-happy gun crews of British and French warships, who at this stage in the Battle of France understandably considered every aircraft they sighted to be hostile. Fortunately, on this occasion at least, their shooting was poor.

Lieutenant Paul Comet, the *Jules Verne*'s navigator, had no difficulty in following his course. The weather was absolutely clear, and excellent visibility enabled him to pick out the island of Sylt from a considerable distance – an important point, for there were heavy anti-aircraft defences on the island and Comet had been worried in case they strayed over them. But Sylt slid harmlessly by away over to the right, and the aircraft flew peacefully on.

The wind forecast had been very precise, allowing Comet to work out an exact ground speed, and after crossing Denmark without incident the *Jules Verne* made landfall on the Baltic coast north of Berlin right on schedule. It was only now that the navigator began to experience some difficulty, because heavy cloud had crept over northern Germany, extending down to about 1,000 feet, and it proved impossible to locate some of the planned landmarks. From time to time, Comet saw the occasional lake through a rift in the cloud, but he was unable to make any positive identification. Then, by sheer good luck, he saw a glow in the sky far ahead: it was Berlin's searchlights. The aircraft's approach must have been detected, and the capital's air-raid defences were now on the alert.

Master Pilot Yonnet steered directly towards the probing searchlight beams. As soon as he reached the suburbs, he flew a series of pre-planned courses over the city, designed to make the Germans think that more than one aircraft was involved with the raid. The *Jules Verne*'s undersides had now been painted matt black and the Germans seemed completely unable to locate the aircraft, despite the dozens of searchlight beams that swept to and fro across the night sky. As yet, not a single anti-aircraft gun had opened up.

Up in the nose of aircraft, Dailliere and Yonnet were finding it increasingly difficult to see. Apart from the glare of the searchlights, more cloud was beginning to drift over Berlin and in just a few more minutes they would be forced to bomb blindly, with the danger of hitting heavily-populated areas. Dailliere therefore ordered the pilot to make for the capital's western suburbs without further delay; intelligence photographs had indicated a cluster of factories in this sector of the city, and these seemed to present the most worthwhile target.

Five minutes later, when he judged that they were directly above the objective – the Farman was fitted with only a rudimentary bomb sight – Dailliere released the two-ton bomb load and ordered Yonnet to set course directly for France. The pilot put down the Farman's nose to gain speed and opened the throttles, anxious to get clear of the city's fringes before the flak started to come up. A few moments later, the clouds reflected the orange flashes of the bomb-bursts, and then the flak started to come up – whole strings of it, twinkling across the Berlin sky. Apart from one or two bursts, most of it was well clear of the Farman, which was not hit.

After the war, the French went to considerable pains to find out if the bombs had hit anything worthwhile, but after the far greater holocaust Berlin had endured by that time this first lone effort had been almost forgotten. Apart from a vague report to the effect that one of the bombs had damaged a factory, German sources indicated that most of the load had fallen in open country.

The homeward flight was made without incident, Yonnet taking the *Jules Verne* in a straight line across western Germany and the Rhine. The aircraft landed at Orly, near Paris, just as dawn was breaking, its fuel reserves practically exhausted.

The *Jules Verne*'s route to Berlin had taken it over Rostock, the home of the Heinkel aircraft factories, and the crew reported that these had been brilliantly lit. The result was that, on the night of 10–11 June, the Farman once again set out for Germany, with Rostock as the target. The objective was reached after a trouble-free flight, although the crew spent several uncomfortable minutes flying round in heavy flak before Dailliere made a satisfactory bombing run. Several fires were reported in the factory area, but again, when the French sought confirmation after the war, no record of any damage could be found in the German files.

Shortly afterwards, the *Jules Verne* was sent to Istres in southern France to take part in operations against the Italians, who had declared war on 10 June. The first mission from this new base, carried out on 14 June, was against oil storage tanks at Porto Marghera, the port of Venice; eight bombs were dropped and at least one tank was definitely set on fire. A second mission, against Leghorn two nights later, was less successful.

The *Jules Verne*'s last sortie was flown on 18 June, when Dailliere and his crew paid a visit to Rome – to drop not bombs but leaflets. Four days later the armistice was signed, and France lay defeated.

Sadly, the big Farman met an inglorious end. Trapped at Marignane through lack of fuel, it was burned to prevent it from falling into enemy hands. Commandant Dailliere, who became a member of the Vichy French forces, was eventually transferred to Dakar in West Africa. One day in 1942, the aircraft he was flying strayed into British territory at Freetown, Sierra Leone, and was shot down by RAF fighters when the pilot apparently ignored signals to land. Dailliere was killed instantly by a bullet through the head.

Such was the tragic death of the man who, with a small band of gallant comrades, carried the war for the first time to Germany's capital in a small, almost personal gesture that shone like a beacon through the shame of France's collapse.

Chapter 4

Kampfgruppe 100: The Luftwaffe's 'Pathfinder Force'

It was November 1940, and the daylight phase of the Battle of Britain was over. The depleted Spitfire and Hurricane squadrons of RAF Fighter Command, exhausted by three months of almost continual operations against the massed formations of the Luftwaffe, now had a breathing-space in which to rest and reequip.

Although the daylight Battle of Britain had ended in victory for the Royal Air Force, the ordeal of Britain's cities was only just beginning. The Luftwaffe, belatedly, had learned the bitter lesson that had been hammered home to RAF Bomber Command nearly a year earlier: that the rate of attrition among bomber formations operating in daylight in an environment where hostile fighters enjoyed superiority was too great to be supported for long.

Since the end of September the Heinkels, Dorniers and Junkers of the Luftwaffe had been coming by night, striking primarily at London, but also ranging across the heart of England to the vital ports of Merseyside, the raids increasing in fury as the weeks went by. There was no question now of restraint; in less than a year, strategic bombing had escalated from semi-precision attacks on legitimate military targets to massive assaults on densely populated centres. The bombing war had become, to a large extent, a psychological onslaught designed to break the morale of the population.

At 8 p.m. on 14 November two squadrons of Heinkel 111 H-3 bombers roared off into the darkness from their base at Vannes, in western France. They crossed the Channel and droned high over the darkened south of England, heading towards their target in the Midlands. Behind them, from a powerful 'Knickebein' transmitter on the French coast, a radio beam lanced out into the night, forming an invisible road in the sky for the aircraft. A steady signal in the pilot's headphones meant that he was on course; dots or dashes meant that he was straying to left or right.

Each bomber was equipped with a special radio receiver known simply as 'X-Apparatus'. A signal, automatically triggered by a second beam cutting across the first at an angle from another 'Knickebein' station, indicated that the bombers were now ten miles from the target. As soon as this signal was received, each radio operator pressed a switch, starting up a clock on his instrument panel. Five miles further on, in response to a signal from a third beam, the radio operator pressed the switch again, stopping the first pointer and starting a second.

It was now up to the pilot to hold the bomber steady on the final run-in to the target. Apart from opening the bomb-doors, that was all he had to do; everything else was automatic. When the second pointer on the radio operator's clock became superimposed on the first, it triggered the electrical bomb-release circuit and the Heinkel leaped as its load of 550-pounders fell away.

On this fateful November night, the target was the lovely cathedral city of Coventry, earmarked by Luftwaffe Intelligence as an important munitions centre and therefore a legitimate military target. During the hours that followed, 450

German bombers, guided by the fires started by the pathfinding Heinkels of Kampfgruppe 100, dropped a total of five hundred tons of high explosive and thirty tons of incendiary bombs into the expanding sea of flame below. When the last wave of bombers droned away in the early hours of 15 November, the heart of Coventry, together with its beautiful fourteenth-century cathedral, had ceased to exist.

Night after night during that desperate winter of 1940–41, London, the Midlands, Lancashire, Wales, Tyneside, Plymouth, Exeter, Southampton, Bristol and many other places reeled under the avalanche of fire from the night sky. Many of the major night raids on England during this period were led by KG 100 and another pathfinder unit, III/KG 28, the Heinkels ranging as far afield as Belfast.

British Intelligence had been aware for some months that the Germans were using radio beams as aids to navigation and bombing. As early as June 1940 Professor Lindemann, the scientific adviser to the British War Cabinet, had reported to Winston Churchill that the Germans had developed a radio beam by means of which they would be able to bomb by day or night, whatever the weather. On 21 June the Prime Minister convened an emergency meeting which was attended by senior RAF officers, scientists and the Deputy Director of Scientific Research at the Air Ministry, Dr R. V. Jones. The latter informed the meeting that for some months hints had been coming in from all sorts of sources on the continent indicating that the Germans had some novel mode of night bombing on which they pinned great hopes. In some way it seemed to be linked with the code name 'Knick-ebein' (Crooked Leg), which British Intelligence had come across several times without being able to explain.

The first theory was that enemy agents had somehow managed to plant radio homing beacons in and around major British targets, but this idea was soon dismissed. Then RAF reconnais-sance aircraft photographed three curiously-shaped towers on the German-occupied coast, structures which did not seem the right shape for any known type of radio or radar transmitter. Soon afterwards, a German bomber was shot down near Liver-pool, and an examination of the wreck revealed that the aircraft carried radio equipment whose elaborate nature suggested that it was connected with something other than the ordinary 'Lorenz' blind-landing system.

From an analysis of this equipment, together with statements made by a captured German airman who broke down under interrogation, Intelligence worked out that the Germans might be planning to navigate and bomb on some sort of radio beam system. At first the idea was received with some incredulity, particularly on the part of senior officers of RAF Bomber Command, whose own crews relied entirely on visual navigation and bombing. Above 20,000 feet, they argued, the stars were nearly always visible, which meant that with thorough training in astro-navigation the bomber crews should be able to find the way to their targets without too much difficulty. What the RAF commanders did not realize at this stage was that only a very small percentage of RAF Bomber Command's crews were accurately locating the target. It would be months before these inaccuracies were fully appreciated and the RAF turned its attention to the development of its own radio navigation system.

Nevertheless, once the British scientists had divined the true purpose of the 'Knickebein' transmitters it did not take the scientists long to devise effective countermeasures against them. On Churchill's orders, priority was given to the erection of radio transmitters along the coast of southern England for the purpose of jamming the enemy beams. The general principle behind the jamming operations was that the countermeasures equipment strengthened the signal from one half of the split beam and not from the other, which meant that an enemy pilot trying to fly so that the signals from both halves of the split beam were equal would stray badly off course.

The first British countermeasures transmitters were operational by the middle of August 1940, their targets being the two 'Ruffian' stations – as the RAF code-named the 'Knickebein' transmitters – near Dieppe and Cherbourg. It was not long before the Germans realized that methods were being tried to jam their stations and they, in turn, took steps to prevent it. During September they installed X-Apparatus, together with new ground and airborne equipment which worked in a different frequency range. By the middle of September the British had discovered enough about the new equipment to design countermeasures, but the necessary jamming equipment could not be produced for another two months, which meant that the Heinkels of KG 100 could carry out their pathfinding operations without interference.

During the last days of October, British Intelligence received indications that the enemy would undertake a large raid with the help of the new equipment before the middle of November, and the assessment was that the target would be either London or Liverpool. This assessment, however, was tragically wrong: the objective of the German experiment was Coventry, where anti-aircraft defences were pitifully light. The enemy lost only one bomber that night.

Meanwhile, the British had devised new airborne radio equipment which enabled aircraft of RAF Bomber Command to fly down the enemy beams and attack the stations which were transmitting them. The first such mission was carried out on the night following the Coventry raid by two Wellingtons of the RAF Wireless Intelligence Unit, one of which achieved a direct hit on the 'Knickebein' station at Cherbourg.

By the beginning of 1941, the British scientists had got the measure of X-Apparatus and countermeasures against it were becoming increasingly effective. In fact, by plotting the direction of the enemy radio beams the British were able to pinpoint targets which were scheduled for attack, with inestimable value to the air defences. Once it was realized that the Luftwaffe intended to attack a target in strength, large decoy fires were lighted some distance away from it, with the result that a large proportion of the total tonnage of enemy bombs fell harmlessly in open country.

Early in 1941, the Germans went over to yet another radio beam system known as Y-Apparatus, again pioneered by the Heinkels of Kampfgruppe 100. Whereas X-Apparatus had used three beams crossing on the approach to the target, Y-Apparatus used only one beam in conjunction with a radio signal which told the bomber pilot how far he was along the beam. By this means the pilot was able to keep a continuous check on his progress, dropping his bombs when the correct distance had been flown. Towards the end of 1942 the RAF was to use a similar system known as 'Oboe', although the latter was a good deal more effective than its earlier German counterpart.

In the case of Y-Apparatus, the main obstacle to its success lay in the fact that British scientists had worked out how it operated even before it became operational, with the result that countermeasures were brought into action from the outset. It was probably due to such countermeasures that enemy bombers attacked Dublin instead of Belfast on the night of 30 May 1941.

Although the weight of the German air offensive against Britain fell off markedly after the end of April 1941, KG 100, now specializing in precision bombing techniques, continued to operate against British targets for several more months. In the summer of 1941 it exchanged some of its Heinkels for Dornier 217s and switched its main effort from land targets to the long series of anti-shipping operations which were to characterize its activities throughout the rest of the war.

In September 1942 several of the Kampfgruppe's most experienced crews were suddenly detached to Germany to take part in trials with two new secret weapons, both of them air-launched radio-guided missiles for use against shipping. The first of these, known as the Fritz-X, consisted of an unpowered 3,100-lb armour-piercing bomb with four stubby fins, spanning 4.6 feet, set midway along its body. The weapon was guided by radio signals and steered by means of a small control column installed in the bomb-aimer's compartment of the launch aircraft.

Immediately after release, the pilot of the parent aircraft reduced speed to about 130 mph, making it easier for the bomb-aimer to keep the missile in sight during the final stages of its trajectory. During the weapon's 42-second drop from 20,000 feet, visual tracking was aided by a flare placed in its tail. The Fritz-X was not very accurate, and its use was complicated by the fact that the launch aircraft – usually a Dornier 217K-2 – had to fly straight and level while course corrections were being made, and this meant that the drop had to be carried out from high altitude to escape the worst of enemy anti-aircraft fire.

When operational trials were completed early in 1943, one of KG 100's squadrons was assigned to Fritz-X operations and sent to Istres, near Marseilles. Under conditions of strict secrecy, stockpiles of Fritz-X missiles were positioned at

German airfields in an arc from northern Norway to Italy, and detachments of KG 100 would shuttle from base to base as the necessity demanded.

Meanwhile, parallel development had continued on the second type of anti-shipping missile, the Henschel Hs 293. Although its armour-piercing capability was not as great as that of the Fritz-X, it was a more flexible weapon in that it could be controlled over a wider range, which was increased by the addition of a rocket motor. This fired automatically after release and accelerated the missile to a speed of 370 mph in twelve seconds. The weapon, which also featured stubby wings and small tail surfaces, was gyroscopically controlled to keep it stable in flight. Like the Fritz-X, it was steered by a small control column in the parent aircraft. Tracking was carried out by means of flare candles fitted to the tail for daylight operations, and a lamp with a red filter for night attacks. From a launch height of 19,500 feet the maximum range of the Hs 293 was 17,500 yards.

In March 1943 Kampfgruppe 100's No. 2 Squadron – II/KG 100 – which had been operating on the Atlantic coast, re-equipped with Dornier 217E-5 bombers and moved to Cognac three months later with its first batch of Hs 293 missiles. On 25 August twelve of its aircraft were ordered to attack Royal Navy warships in the Bay of Biscay. On this occasion, each bomber carried two Hs 293s, one under each wing. Three British vessels were sighted and in the resulting attack one corvette was damaged. Two days later, during a second attack, the missile-armed bombers sank the corvette HMS *Egret* in the same area and damaged a destroyer.

On 7 September 1943 II/KG 100 joined its Fritz-X-equipped sister squadron, III/KG 100, at Istres and the two units were immediately ordered into action against the Allied bridgehead at Salerno in Italy. Because of complete Allied air superiority, the Dorniers were forced to operate at night and there was no confirmation of any hits by the missiles. Operations in the Salerno area were brought to a halt on 18 September as the lack of moonlight was making it increasingly difficult to aim the bombs with any degree of accuracy.

Those hectic days of September 1943 saw KG 100 take part in some of the most noteworthy attack missions carried out by Luftwaffe bombers during the entire war. On the ninth, the day when the Allies went ashore at Salerno, III/KG 100 was presented with a once-in-a-lifetime target. Early that morning, German reconnaissance revealed that major units of the Italian fleet were at sea off the west coast of Italy. The Italian Government had already capitulated, and the future of the fleet was uncertain. If it went over to the Allies, it could conceivably lend weight to their already over-whelming naval supremacy in the Mediterranean; on the other hand, if it sailed for harbours in southern France it would provide major reinforce-ments for the small German naval presence there. Accordingly, the order went out to III/KG 100: if the Italian fleet sailed north, it was to be protected; if it sailed south, it was to be sunk.

A couple of hours later the Germans received the news that the Italian fleet had in fact turned south. Three battleships, six cruisers and a whole armada of escort vessels were apparently heading towards Malta to surrender. The battleships were the *Vittorio Veneto*, the *Italia* and the *Roma*, the last-named a giant of 42,500 tons mounting nine 15-inch guns. In just a few hours they would be within range of the Allied fighter umbrella that would ensure their safety on the voyage; if action was to be taken against them, it had to be immediate.

At 2 p.m., two Dornier 217s – the only two in readiness – took off from Istres, each carrying one Fritz-X and a full fuel load. For an hour they flew low across the Mediterranean to avoid the Allied radar, then climbed to 18,000 feet. Soon afterwards they sighted the Italian fleet steaming in loose formation and the first bursts of flak started to come up. In the leading aircraft, Oberleutnant Heinrich Schmetz selected the battleship *Roma* as his target, releasing the missile and then reducing speed to 130 mph while the bombardier tracked its flight. The battleship began evasive action with a wide turn, but Schmetz's bomb-aimer, Feld-webel Oscar Huhn, kept the white flare in the Fritz-X's tail directly superimposed on the ship's foredeck. At 3:40 there was a red flash as the missile made a direct hit, ripping the ship's vitals apart in a terrific explosion. In less than twenty minutes the *Roma* had vanished beneath the surface, killing 1,254 Italian sailors, including the Italian fleet commander, Admiral Carlos Bergamini.

Schmetz was awarded the Knight's Cross for his part in the operation, while his bomb-aimer received the Iron Cross. Schmetz was later appointed to command III/KG 100.

It was not until after the war, however, that the true nature of this operation became known. The Luftwaffe High Command forbade the release of the news that the battleship had been sunk by a missile, implying that ordinary armour-piercing bombs had done the job. This was apparently to preserve secrecy, but there was an internal reason too. Not even Göring was informed, for senior Luftwaffe officers were afraid that if the news of the successes registered by the air-to-surface missiles reached the ears of Adolf Hitler he would attempt to turn the Fritz-X into another 'wonder weapon' and call for the mass production of the bombers capable of launching it, to the detriment of the fighters which Germany so badly needed.

The next few days saw the crews of III/KG 30 operating intensively against the Salerno bridge-head, pressing home their missile attacks against Allied warships. The Germans had to fly through heavy flak and fighter cover and losses were high, but thirty per cent of the missiles launched found their targets. On 16 September 1943 three Fritz-X missiles were launched against the British battleship

HMS *Warspite*; one of them tore through several decks to blast a hole in the ship's bottom while the other two achieved very near misses, cutting a long tear in *Warspite*'s side compartments, destroying one boiler-room completely and flooding four out of the remaining five.

Only nine men were killed and fourteen wounded, but the battleship was completely out of action, unable to steer and with her radar and armament rendered unserviceable. She shipped 5,000 tons of water and for some time it was touch and go whether she would float or not. She was laboriously towed back to Malta for repairs, and it was to be several months before she saw action again. Other missile hits were scored on the cruisers HMS *Uganda* and USS *Savannah*, as well as on a number of freighters. From now on, however, III/KG 100's operations were severely curtailed as the Allies established airstrips in the Salerno area, enabling fighters to maintain constant patrols over the beachhead.

KG 100 had now been joined by a second missile-launching unit, KG 40, which suffered badly from a shortage of fuel and experienced aircrew and, most of all, from the type of aircraft it flew. These were Heinkel He 177 heavy bombers, which suffered badly from engine trouble. The machine was powered by four Daimler-Benz DB 610A in-line engines, mounted side by side in pairs and coupled to drive a single propeller shaft, so that the bomber had a twin-engined appearance. It was heartily disliked by its crews, who nicknamed it 'Flaming Coffin' because of its habit of bursting into flames without warning.

In January 1944 both units were in action against the Allied landings at Anzio, south of Rome, with attacks carried out by 25 Dornier 217s of KG 100 and a similar number of Heinkel 177s from KG 40. In a week of operations the German squadrons suffered fifty per cent losses to the strong fighter cover over the beachhead. In addition, the Allied warships were now using effective countermeasures, including a radio jammer known as CXGE which jammed the enemy's missile guidance system. Nevertheless, the missiles did succeed in hitting the cruiser HMS *Spartan*, which capsized and sank within minutes after sustaining two hits.

In the spring of 1944, with an Allied invasion of France a distinct possibility during the coming months, KG 100 was once more transferred to bases on the Atlantic coast for operations against Allied shipping. On 30 April, III/KG 100 used Fritz-X missiles for the first and only time against the United Kingdom when fifteen Dornier 217s released the weapons against shipping in Plymouth Harbour. No important target was hit.

All the missile-equipped Luftwaffe units were assembled to counteract the Allied invasion when it finally came in June 1944, and it had been expected that they would wreak a great deal of havoc among the densely-packed shipping between the coasts of England and France. The Luftwaffe High Command, however, had reckoned without total Allied air superiority, which made anti-shipping attacks completely impossible during daylight. Operations were just as hazardous at night, the bombers having to run the gauntlet of their own German coastal flak as well as the Allied night-fighters and anti-aircraft guns on the beach-heads and the warships offshore. Few of the crews managed to press home their attacks, and no major success was achieved.

In mid-July, the surviving aircraft and crews were transferred to bases in Norway and Germany, where they reverted to anti-shipping attacks with conventional bombs until their disbandment in the autumn. For the unit that had once sown the whirlwind when it lit the fires that razed Coventry, and since then had pioneered a new era of aerial warfare, it was an undistinguished ending.

Chapter 5

By Daylight to Germany

For RAF Bomber Command, the early weeks of 1941 marked the beginning of a significant new phase in the air war. On the night of 10–11 February, four-engined heavy bombers of the RAF were used operationally for the first time when Short Stirlings of No. 7 Squadron bombed oil storage tanks at Rotterdam, and a few nights later a second new heavy bomber type, the twin-engined Avro Manchester, made its operational debut when six aircraft of No. 207 Squadron attacked an enemy cruiser in Brest harbour. Then, on the night of 11–12 March, No. 35 Squadron's new four-engined Handley-Page Halifax bombers made their first venture over enemy territory, bombing the ports of Le Havre and Dieppe.

Much of Bomber Command's effort during the spring of 1941 was, in fact, directed against the French Atlantic ports and the German capital ships assembled there: the *Scharnhorst*, *Gneisenau* and *Prinz Eugen*, recognized by the British War Cabinet as the greatest potential source of danger to the island's vital Atlantic supply convoys. The large number of night sorties flown against the warships, however, produced little result, and there was a general feeling among the leaders of Bomber Command that the tonnage of bombs wasted could have been put to far better effect in attacks on the big industrial complexes of western Germany.

Several fairly large-scale night attacks were carried out on targets in Germany between March and May 1941, the biggest on the night of 8–9 May when 360 aircraft were sent out to attack Hamburg and Bremen, but the results were still disappointing. Crews were still having to navigate and bomb visually, and many of them were failing to locate the target. In many cases, crews were reporting successful attacks, with attendant severe damage, only for post-raid reconnaissance to show that the target was untouched.

Gradually, although the idea was opposed strongly by the RAF Group Commanders whose bombers had suffered fearfully in the disastrous daylight raids of late 1939, Bomber Command's thinking once more turned to the possibility of daylight raids on enemy targets. These thoughts were influenced by two events in particular: the German invasion of the Balkans in April 1941, and the assault on the Soviet Union in June, both of which had led to the transfer of several elite Luftwaffe fighter groups from the western front. The British Air Staff believed that if the enemy could be persuaded to pull more fighter units out of Germany, and concentrate them on the Channel coast to replace those sent east, then daylight penetration raids into Germany might have a chance of success. It was decided, therefore, to mount a series of strong and co-ordinated fighter and bomber attacks on objectives in the area immediately across the Channel, in the hope that these would persuade the enemy to withdraw fighter units from the air defence of Germany and station them on the Pas de Calais airfields.

These attacks, known as 'Circus' operations, got into their stride in June 1941 with small numbers of bombers escorted by several squadrons of fighters carrying out daylight raids on enemy airfields and supply dumps in France. Most of the bombers involved were the twin-engined Bristol Blenheims of Bomber Command's No. 2 Group, but heavy bombers were occasionally involved; on 19 July, for example, Stirlings of No. 7 Squadron, strongly escorted by Spitfires, bombed targets in the vicinity of Dunkirk.

Meanwhile, by the end of June, it had been decided that the 'Circus' operations were keeping sufficient numbers of enemy fighters pinned down to enable RAF bombers to make unescorted daylight penetrations into Germany, and on the last day of the month Halifax heavy bombers of No. 35 Squadron made a daylight attack on Kiel. All returned to base without loss.

On that same day the Blenheims of No. 2 Group had also been standing by to attack an important target in northern Germany: the port of Bremen, or more specifically the shipyards in the harbour area. These yards were responsible for roughly a quarter of Germany's U-boat production, and at a time when enemy submarines were taking a fearful toll of British shipping in the Atlantic the importance of precision bombing attacks on such objectives could not be overestimated. The problem was that the yards actually producing the submarines were extremely difficult to locate at night, and although several night raids had already been carried out on Bremen there was no evidence that submarine production had been affected in the slightest. To achieve the necessary identification and accuracy an attack would have to be made in broad daylight, and Bremen was one of the most heavily-defended targets in Europe, protected by a forest of barrage balloons and anti-aircraft guns of every calibre.

The dangerous and difficult mission was assigned to Nos 105 and 107 Squadrons of No. 2 Group, both equipped with Blenheim Mk IV bombers. The Blenheim had been the RAF's standard medium bomber since 1937, and when it first appeared it was about 40 mph faster than most fighters then in service. By 1940, however, things had changed, and the type had suffered terrible losses during unescorted daylight missions in the Battle of France. The Mk IV was the latest, greatly improved version. Powered by two Bristol Mercury radial engines, it had a top speed of 266 mph at 11,800 feet and its maximum range was 1,460 miles. It carried a bomb load of 1,000 lbs and a defensive armament of five .303 Browning machine-guns. Each Blenheim carried a crew of three: pilot, navigator/bomb-aimer and wireless operator/air-gunner. The last-named sat in a turret on top of the fuselage, behind two of the machine-guns; there were two more guns in a turret under the nose, operated by the navigator, and the fifth gun, which was fixed and fired forwards, was operated by the pilot.

The Blenheims had already made one attempt to reach Bremen, on 28 June, but as they approached the enemy coast the sky ahead had revealed itself to be brilliantly blue, without a trace of cloud cover, and the formation leader – Wing Commander Laurence Petley, commanding No. 107 Squadron – had quite rightly ordered his aircraft to turn back. Petley was an old hand, and knew that if the Blenheims pressed on they would have little chance of survival without cloud to shelter in if they were attacked by fighters; in fact, they would probably not even reach the target.

Now, on the thirtieth, the Blenheims set out for the target once more, this time led by Wing Commander Hughie Edwards of No. 105 Squadron. Edwards, an athletic six-footer aged twenty-seven, had been born in Fremantle, Australia on 1 August 1914, the son of a Welsh immigrant family. After his schooling he had worked in a shipping office, a steady but boring job which he left to join the Australian Army as a private in 1934. A few months later he obtained a transfer to the Royal Australian Air Force, and in 1936 he was transferred yet again, this time to the RAF. The beginning of 1938 had found him at RAF Station Bicester, flying Blenheim Mk Is with No. 90 Squadron; to be the pilot of what was then Britain's fastest bomber was the fulfilment of all his dreams.

Then, in August 1938, shortly after his twenty-fourth birthday, came disaster. The Blenheim he was flying became caught in severe icing conditions, spinning down out of control through dense cloud. Edwards baled out, but his parachute fouled the aircraft's rudder and he was only a few hundred feet off the ground by the time he managed to free himself. He suffered severe injuries in the resultant heavy landing, the most serious of which was the severing of the main nerve in his right leg, causing paralysis from the knee down.

He spent the next two years in and out of hospital and was told that he would never fly again, but his dogged persistence refused to accept the fact and in August 1940 he regained his full flying category. He had not long been back with his old squadron at Bicester, however, when bad luck caught him out again. Returning to base after a night-flying exercise on a black, moonless night, he found that an enemy air raid was in progress and all the airfield lighting had been switched off. Unable to land in the pitch darkness, he was forced to fly round in circles until his fuel ran out, whereupon he ordered his crew members to bail out. Then he tried to follow suit – only to find that his escape hatch was jammed, trapping him inside the aircraft. He brought the Blenheim down in a flat glide, flying as slowly as possible, and waited for the impact. A few moments later the bomber slammed through the branches of a tree, hit the ground and broke up, leaving Edwards sitting in the remains of the cockpit with no worse injury than concussion.

The accident, however, delayed the start of his operational career until February 1941, when he flew his first missions with No. 139 Squadron. He at once began to make up for lost time with a series of daring raids, usually at low level, over occupied France. The casualty rate was high, and for those who survived promotion was rapid. It was not long before Edwards was posted to command No. 105 Squadron with the rank of Wing Commander, and by the last week of June 1941 he had thirty-five operational sorties to his credit.

Edwards had studied the Bremen defences until he knew their layout by heart, and he knew they could not be penetrated by normal methods. There was only one way to approach and bomb the target, and that was at low level. In this way, with the element of surprise on their side, some of the attacking crews might just have a chance of getting through. Edwards, however, was under no illusions; operating at very low level meant increased fuel consumption, and even with full tanks the Blenheims would just have enough fuel to make the round trip. If something unforeseen cropped up, such as a strong unexpected headwind on the way back, they might not be able to make it home.

The attempt of 30 June, however, like the one two days earlier, was doomed to failure. Fifteen Blenheims from the two squadrons took off that morning from their base at Swanton Morley in clear weather conditions, but as they crossed the North Sea it was apparent that the weather was deteriorating rapidly. The enemy coast was shrouded in a blanket of dense fog, and although the formation pressed on for several minutes through the grey wall Edwards soon knew that it was hopeless. Only two bombers had managed to keep station with him; the others were scattered in the murk and hopelessly lost. He ordered his wireless operator to tap out the recall signal, and the widely dispersed bombers came straggling back to their Norfolk base in ones and twos.

Early on 4 July the fifteen bombers made a third attempt. Bremen had been bombed the previous night, and it was hoped that this attack might have caused some disruption of the German defences, giving the Blenheims an extra chance.

The bombers – nine aircraft from No. 105 Squadron and six from No. 107 – made rendezvous over the Norfolk coast and set course in tight vics of three, flying at fifty feet over the waves, their slipstream furrowing the sparkling water as they followed the luminous pathway made by the rays of the rising sun. Edwards' plan was to skirt the shipping lanes near the Frisian Islands and the North German coast, turning in to make a landfall west of Cuxhaven and then making a slight detour to avoid the outer flak defences of Bremerhaven before making a fast, straight-in approach to Bremen.

Edwards was aware that however careful they were, they were bound to be detected by enemy shipping before they reached the enemy coast. Speed and surprise were essential to the attack plan, and as the formation approached the Frisians Edwards increased speed to a fast cruise of 230 mph, sacrificing fuel reserves in a bid to increase the all-important surprise element. The speed increase, however, proved too much for three of the 107 Squadron aircraft; unable to keep up, they gradually lost contact with the rest of the formation, and their pilots, realizing the folly of continuing, turned for home.

The remaining twelve thundered on, still skimming the surface of the sea. Edwards' navigator, Pilot Officer Ramsay, reported that they were north of Cuxhaven and told the pilot to steer on a new heading of 180 degrees, due south towards the mouth of the River Weser. A few moments later, as the Blenheims approached the German coastline, a number of dark shapes suddenly loomed up out of the morning haze. They were merchant ships, and in seconds they had flashed beneath the wings of the speeding bombers. The damage, however, had been done. The ships would already be signalling a warning of the Blenheims' approach – unless, Edwards thought optimistically, the enemy crews had mistaken them for a squadron of Junkers 88 returning from a mission. The Blenheim and the Ju 88 bore a superficial resemblance to one another, and this had often led to confusion in the past, sometimes with fatal results.

The bombers drummed over the coast and raced on in a thunderclap of sound over the flat, drab countryside of northern Germany. Edwards had a fleeting glimpse of a horse and cart careering into a ditch in confusion as the Blenheims roared over-head, and of white upturned faces as the people in the fields waved at them, doubtless mistaking them for friendly aircraft. In the mid-upper gun turret, the gunner, Flight Sergeant Jerry Quinn, had no eyes for the scenery; he was busy scanning the sky above and to left and right, searching for the first sign of the enemy fighters he was certain must be speeding to intercept them.

Bremerhaven slid by off the bombers' starboard wingtips, a dark smudge under its curtain of indus-trial haze. A railway line flashed under them, and

Edwards picked out the town of Oldenburg away on the right, in the distance. Then, leaning forward in his seat to peer ahead, he picked out a dense cluster of silvery dots, standing out against the blue summer sky. Each one of those dots was a barrage balloon, and in a few more minutes the twelve Blenheims would have to weave their way through the middle of them, into the inferno of the flak barrage that lay beyond.

In order to present more problems to the enemy anti-aircraft gunners Edwards ordered his pilots to attack in line abreast, with a couple of hundred yards' spacing between each aircraft. The Blenheims of 107 Squadron took up station on the left of the line, with 105 Squadron on the right. The bomber on the extreme left was flown by Wing Commander Petley, who had led the abortive raid of 28 June.

The bombers stuck doggedly to their course as they sped into the forest of barrage balloons. Whether they got through or not was largely a matter of luck; any pilot who took evasive action to miss a cable risked plunging into one of the tall cranes or pylons that cluttered the harbour area. Yet, miraculously, they all did get through, thundering like a whirlwind over the drab grey streets, the wharves and the warehouses. All around them now, the sky erupted in fire and steel as German anti-aircraft gunners ashore and on the ships around the harbour pumped thousands of shells into their path, and the shellfire began to take its inevitable toll. A Blenheim turned lazily over on its back and ploughed into a street, exploding in a great wave of burning petrol. A second blew up in mid-air as a shell tore into its bomb-bay. A third, one wing torn off, cartwheeled into a group of warehouses and pulverized them in the explosion of its bombs.

On the left flank of the formation, Wing Commander Petley's Blenheim suddenly pulled up into a climb, flames streaming from its engines. It turned, as though the pilot were desperately trying to regain control and seek somewhere to land, but a few moments later it plunged vertically into a sports field.

The rest raced on, over streets filled with panic-stricken people who scattered for shelter from the sleet of shrapnel that poured down on them from their own anti-aircraft guns, a greater menace to individuals than the bombers roaring overhead. Every bomber was hit time after time, shell splinters and bullets ripping through wings and fuselage. Then they darted into the vast, sprawling docks area, each pilot selecting his individual target among the complex of factories, sheds, warehouses and wharves that lay in his path. From this height, it was virtually impossible to miss. The Blenheims lurched and jolted violently in the shock-waves as the explosions of their bombs sent columns of debris hurtling hundreds of feet into the air. Clouds of smoke boiled up, obscuring the harbour, as the bombers plunged on through the outer ring of defences, all of them still taking hits.

The worst of the flak was behind them now, but the danger was not yet over. Still flying at fifty feet, Edwards was suddenly horrified to see a line of high tension cables directly in his path. Acting instinctively, he eased the control column forward a fraction and dipped underneath them, the bomber's wingtip scraping past a pylon with only a couple of feet to spare. Seconds later, the Blenheim lurched as it sped over a road; it had flown slap through some telephone wires.

The eight surviving bombers raced for the sanctuary of the coast, leapfrogging over woods and villages. Every aircraft was holed like a sieve, and many of the crew members were wounded. They included Gerry Quinn, Edwards' gunner, who had a shell splinter in his knee. One Blenheim had yards of telephone wire trailing from its tail wheel. All the aircraft returned to base, but many of them were so badly damaged that they had to be scrapped.

For his part in leading the attack, Hughie Edwards received the award of the Victoria Cross. His navigator received the DFC, and Gerry Quinn a Bar to his Distinguished Flying Medal. Members of several other crews were also decorated.

There was no denying that the Bremen raid had been a very gallant effort, with enormous propaganda value at a time when Britain was suffering serious reverses in the Western Desert and the Atlantic, but the damage inflicted on the target hardly justified the fact that thirty-three per cent of the attacking force had been lost over Bremen. Taking into account the Blenheims that had to be written off later because of battle damage, this figure climbed to sixty per cent.

Nevertheless, the fact that no enemy fighters had made an appearance during the attack seemed encouraging enough for the Air Staff to authorize further missions of this kind. Meanwhile, daylight attacks continued against the warships in the French Atlantic ports. The biggest of these missions to date was mounted on 24 July, when RAF heavy and medium bombers raided Brest harbour. This attack was noteworthy because it involved the use of American-built Boeing B-17 Fortress Is, twenty of which had recently been purchased by the RAF and pressed into service with No. 90 Squadron. The Fortresses had flown their first operational mission on 8 July, when three of them set out to raid Wilhelmshaven by daylight. Two of them bombed the target from an altitude of 30,000 feet and the third, experiencing engine trouble, bombed the island of Norderney before turning back. Three more Fortresses were to have bombed Berlin on the twenty-third, but this mission had to be abandoned because of bad weather.

Now, on the following day, three of 90 Squadron's Fortresses each dropped four 1,000-lb bombs on Brest from 32,000 feet, the highest attack so far carried out by any bombers. They were followed by ninety-nine twin-engined bombers, mainly Vickers Wellingtons with a small number of Handley-Page Hampdens, which flew through intense flak to bomb Brest from medium altitude.

As the bombers turned for home they were savagely attacked by German fighters, but it was the highly accurate anti-aircraft fire which accounted for most of the thirteen bombers that failed to return.

Meanwhile, Stirlings and Halifaxes had battled their way through strong fighter opposition to attack the port of La Pallice, where the battle cruiser *Scharnhorst* was sheltering. The fighters destroyed one of the six Stirlings that took part, but all the rest suffered damage and some limped back to base in a pitiful condition, their crews dead and dying inside the bloodstained, shell-torn fuselages. The fourteen Halifaxes were even worse hit; they were engaged by two squadrons of Messerschmitt 109s, which shot down five of them and damaged all the rest. Nevertheless, the Halifaxes' bombs scored five hits on the warship, causing serious damage. That night, she limped up the coast to join her sister ships in Brest.

It was becoming clear that daylight bombers could only hope to attack strongly defended targets without suffering severe losses if they had the benefit of massive fighter escort, or alternatively if the attacks could be made at sufficiently high altitude. Only the Boeing Fortress, which seemed to have the ability to outclimb enemy fighters above 30,000 feet, fitted the latter requirement, and Bomber Command entertained hopes that the aircraft might be used to make high-level precision attacks on targets deep inside Germany.

On 26 July two Fortresses set out to bomb Hamburg, but the mission was frustrated by bad weather. One returned to base with its bombs still on board, and the other bombed Emden from 32,000 feet through scattered cloud. A week later, a solitary Fortress dropped four thousand-pounders on Kiel; it was attacked by enemy fighters at 32,000 feet – the first time a Fortress had been engaged by the enemy – and suffered some damage before making its escape. The Fortress's gunners were unable to return the enemy fire because their weapons were frozen solid.

On 12 August, two more Fortresses bombed Cologne and Emden from altitudes in excess of 33,000 feet. These raids formed part of a whole series of diversionary attacks on targets in occupied Europe undertaken by Bomber Command that day, covered by a total of 1,500 aircraft of Fighter Command. The attacks were designed to divert the enemy's attention from the deepest daylight penetration carried out by Bomber Command so far – a daring low-level attack by fifty-four Blenheims of No. 2 Group on two power stations near Cologne. On this occasion, the Blenheims – six squadrons in all – were escorted by the twin-engined Westland Whirlwind fighters of No. 263 Squadron, which accompanied them as far as Antwerp. Had the Whirlwind been available in large numbers, its employment as an escort fighter might have made a profound difference to Bomber Command's daylight bombing policy. It was fast, highly manoeuvrable and extremely well armed with four 20-mm cannon in the nose, but it suffered from continual trouble with its Rolls-Royce Peregrine engines and the only two squadrons equipped with it, after carrying out a small number of escort missions, went over to ground-attack work until they re-equipped with Hawker Typhoons in 1943.

Two days after the mission of 12 August two of 90 Squadron's Fortresses were bombing Brest from 35,000 feet when they were attacked by at least seven enemy fighters. They latched on to one of the Fortresses and made no fewer than twenty-six separate attacks on it, chasing it until it was thirty miles off the English coast. The crippled bomber staggered over the cliffs at five hundred feet and crash-landed near Plymouth, killing three of its crew.

In all, the Fortresses flew fifty-one high-altitude missions against targets in Germany and occupied Europe; half of them had to be completely abandoned because of frozen guns, engine failure at altitude, bad weather in the target area or the forming of condensation trails behind the bombers, leading fighters unerringly to them. Of the fifty tons of bombs they dropped, about forty-nine tons, according to RAF Intelligence reports, fell wide of the target. Three Fortresses were destroyed by enemy action, two of them when they were intercepted by a strong force of Messerschmitt 109s during a mission against the German battleship *Admiral Scheer* in Oslo harbour on 8 September. Four more Fortresses were lost accidentally, two of them when they literally fell apart during high-level training flights. Their unfortunate crews had learned to their cost about a phenomenon which was at that time an unknown quantity: severe clear-air turbulence in the vicinity of high-altitude, high-speed winds, or 'jet streams' as they were later to be known.

No. 90 Squadron ceased operations with its Fortresses over Europe at the end of September 1941, and later re-equipped with Short Stirlings. The Fortress had proved a bitter disappointment, not because there was much wrong with the bomber's design, but because high-altitude daylight bombing was a new science which required much more expertise, and much better equipment, before it could be undertaken successfully.

Nevertheless, the RAF's early and short-lived Fortress operations were a taste of things to come two years later, when improved B-17 Flying Fortresses of the mighty United States Eighth Air Force would spin vapour trails in their hundreds over the devastated cities and industries of the Third Reich.

Chapter 6

The Raid that Ran Out of Fuel

On a wartime bomber station, it was always fairly certain that the ground crews could guess the nature of the night's target hours before the aircrew were briefed. The reason was simple; the ground crews were the men responsible for fuelling and arming the bombers. A lot of bombs and reduced fuel load meant a target in occupied France, Belgium or Holland; fewer bombs and more fuel meant the Ruhr Valley; while maximum fuel and minimum bomb load denoted an objective somewhere deep in the heart of Germany, at the limit of the bombers' range.

On the afternoon of 7 November 1941 ground crews on the RAF's bomber bases in Yorkshire and East Anglia looked at one another knowingly. It was maximum fuel, minimum bombs. This was the trip the aircrew hated: Berlin.

It was to be a maximum-effort raid, the biggest so far against Germany's capital city, with bombers drawn from Bomber Command's Nos 1, 3, 4 and 5 Groups, and it had been projected for some time. Now, at last, the date had been fixed; the raid would take place on the night of 7–8 November.

There were a great many attendant problems, not the least of which was the weather. For the past few days, Bomber Command's meteorologists had been striving to build up a picture of probable weather conditions over the route to the target and Berlin itself on the night in question, and their forecast was far from optimistic. Large cloud formations were building up over Germany, their tops rising to altitudes of more than 20,000 feet, and there was a strong probability of thunderstorms, hail and severe icing. To complicate matters even further, westerly winds were expected to increase in strength during the evening, meeting the bombers head-on as they battled their way home. Even Bomber Command's new four-engined 'heavies', the Stirlings and Halifaxes, would find the going hard enough: but the majority of the bombers earmarked for the raid were twin-engined Wellingtons, Whitleys and

Hampdens, the 'old guard' of the RAF's bomber force.

Despite the apparent difficulties, the planners of Bomber Command's Nos 1, 3, 4 and 5 Groups, conferring over their telephone links and assessing the weather forecast of the morning of the raid, decided that everything should go ahead. Nevertheless, some of the group commanders were far from happy, and the unhappiest of them all was Air Vice-Marshal John Slessor, the Air Officer Commanding No. 5 Group, whose squadrons of elderly Handley-Page Hampdens stood to suffer the biggest loss of all under adverse conditions.

Slessor had been away on a visit to Bomber Command HQ during the morning and early afternoon of 7 November, and when he returned to his own Group Headquarters – a large rambling house known as St Vincents in the Lincolnshire town of Grantham – he found his senior meteorological officer, Mr Matthews, waiting for him in a state of considerable agitation. Matthews told Slessor, in the strongest possible terms, that to send the Hampdens on the 1,200-mile round trip to Berlin in severe icing conditions would entail quite unacceptable risks. Although the Hampden was faster than either the Whitley or Wellington, it was prone to severe airframe icing. Hampden crews also suffered badly during prolonged flights in intense cold, particularly the rear-gunners, who sat on top of the tadpole-like fuselage under an open cupola. They often had to be helped from their cramped stations, literally frozen stiff, the tears caused by the biting airflow frozen into a mask of ice over their faces.

Slessor listened carefully to Matthews, and agreed with him. He decided at once to exercise his group commander's privilege and alter the target. The Hampdens of No. 5 Group would go to the Ruhr, Oslo, Cologne, Ostend and Boulogne that night, instead of Berlin.

Some station commanders in the other groups received news of the target with dismay. Berlin was a difficult and dangerous trip at the most favourable of times, but now it looked as though their aircraft would have to battle home through ice and cloud, in the face of savage headwinds and severe turbulence. The station commanders, however, had no choice in the matter. Orders from Group HQ were final. All they could do was to select their most experienced crews to take part in the raid, realizing that the new boys would have far less chance of coming through.

In all, 169 crews of Nos 1, 3 and 4 Groups were briefed to attack Berlin. Fifty-five more were scheduled to carry out a diversionary raid on Mannheim. The crews scheduled to hit Berlin were advised to land on airfields in southern England after the raid, as their fuel on return would be marginal.

As darkness fell on 7 November, the Yorkshire and Lincolnshire bomber airfields resounded to the thunder of engines as the Whitleys and Wellingtons – together with a smaller number of Stirlings, Halifaxes and Manchesters – climbed away into the cold gloom, labouring under their loads of bombs and fuel. As they droned out over the North Sea and across the enemy coast, the bomber crews found to their consternation that the cloud conditions were even worse than they had been led to expect. The cloud tops towered up to 25,000 feet and even higher, which left the crews with two equally depressing alternatives. Either they could fly through the clouds and risk the inevitable icing, or they could re-route their flight around them and use up additional quantities of their precious fuel.

The experience of one crew, flying a Whitley bomber of No. 10 Squadron from Dishforth, in North Yorkshire, was typical. On the flight outward over the North Sea they climbed to 21,000 feet, just clear of the cloud tops, but ahead of them they saw more clouds barring their path. The pilot decided to go around them, and when the Whitley crossed the Danish coast the clouds had begun to break up. By this time, however, the aircraft had used up so much fuel that it was pointless trying to reach Berlin; the bomber would never make it home. The pilot therefore turned south, looking for a clear spot through which they could drop their bombs on some worthwhile target. After searching for some time, the navigator sighted Lübeck through a gap in the clouds and unloaded the bombs.

The pilot decided he had enough fuel left to fly directly home to Dishforth, but by now the dense cloud extended over the whole of the North Sea. Luckily, he found a small gap just off the western coast of Denmark and descended in a tight spiral, levelling out only five hundred feet above the sea. He brought the bomber all the way home at this height, battling through thunderstorms whose severe turbulence tossed the aircraft around the sky like a cork and threading his way through the valleys of the North Yorkshire moors to make a safe landing at three o'clock in the morning. It was a miserable crew that staggered from the bowels of the aircraft, white-faced, frozen to the marrow and stained with their own vomit.

Many other crews had a similar experience, choosing alternative targets such as Lübeck, Rostock, Warnemünde, Kiel, Schleswig and Sylt. They were the lucky ones, for they had sufficient reserves of fuel to reach their home bases. Yet for most, the flight back was a nerve-racking business, their bombers skimming the choppy, inhospitable sea at heights as low as three hundred feet. Almost every crew underwent terrible airsickness, no matter how experienced they were.

For the crews who decided to try and reach Berlin, the outward flight was a nightmare. They had no alternative, for reasons of conserving fuel, but to push on through cloud, and before long the accumulation of ice on the wings forced the bombers to descend into the depths of the murk. Some, before they shed their burden of ice, broke through the cloud base and found themselves flying over northern Germany at less than five hundred feet; others, trapped in the cloud, had no hope of finding the target and turned for home with their bombs still on board.

Others, by a combination of good luck and expert flying, managed to reach the German capital. One of them was the crew of a Whitley of No. 102 Squadron from Topcliffe, in Yorkshire, just up the road from No. 10's base at Dishforth. The pilot was Sergeant Tony Whickham, who bombed Berlin through one of the few gaps in the cloud and then turned for home, pursued by some scattered light flak. On the way back, still over German territory, the Whitley was blown badly off course when a big increase in wind strength made nonsense of the navigator's careful calculations. The bomber strayed over Hamburg, where it was greeted by an intense flak barrage. Whickham took evasive action and got clear, but over the Dutch coast the aircraft encountered a massive bank of cumulo-nimbus cloud. Because fuel was running low Whickham had no alternative but to plunge into it, holding his course. A few minutes later both engines began to ice up, and soon afterward they cut out altogether.

The crew, very frightened, sat there in the unreal silence while the pilot took the Whitley down in a fast glide from 12,000 to 2,000 feet. As they got lower, great chunks of ice flew from the wings and propellers, hammering against the fuselage with a fearful noise. At 2,000 feet, with the crew preparing for a ditching in the icy sea, the engines coughed and suddenly burst into full-throated life. Whickham, completely exhausted by the ordeal of controlling the ponderous bomber, nevertheless brought her home to a safe landing after flying across the North Sea at three hundred feet. He and his crew were lucky; some No. 102 Squadron pilots were so worn out that they misjudged their landing and crashed. One Whitley bounced, careered off the runway and ploughed through some Nissen huts, killing several airmen who were sleeping there.

For many of the crews cold was the main ordeal. As they droned on through the freezing overcast towards Berlin, temperatures inside the bombers fell to more than sixty degrees below zero, and any crew member who touched a metal part without his gloves risked instant frostbite. Frost coated the interiors of the vibrating fuselages and formed on the faces of the men. For long periods the aircraft flew blindly, their windscreens covered with an opaque white layer. Some of the more experienced crews had brought glycerine with them, which they dabbed on the windows to disperse the internal ice.

Amid the blinding, icy darkness, there were stories of heroism as individual aircraft fought their way to the target. One of them, a Wellington of No. 3 Group, arrived over Berlin and dropped its cargo of high-explosive bombs through a rift in the clouds, but the murk closed in again before its incendiaries could be released. The pilot therefore decided to keep them on board in the hope that they would spot a worthwhile target on the homeward flight.

It turned out to be an unfortunate decision. While still above Germany, the Wellington was hit in the bomb-bay by an anti-aircraft shell and its load of incendiaries set alight. Shell splinters smashed the bomb-release mechanism, and in less than a minute the aircraft's bomb-bay was ablaze from end to end. The crew used every available fire extinguisher in a vain attempt to put the fire out, and when the contents of the extinguishers ran out they used coffee from their flasks. The flames burst up into the fuselage, eating away the fabric and exposing the metal frames of the bomber's geodetic construction. The rear-gunner was trapped in his turret, completely isolated from the other members of the crew, and since the intercom was out of action he toyed with the idea of baling out. Then, realizing that the aircraft was still holding a steady course, he decided to stay where he was for the time being.

During all this time flak shells continued to burst around the bomber. Its bomb-doors were open and the pilot, realizing that the trail of fire spewing from the aircraft's belly must look like a beacon to the enemy gunners, decided to close them. It was a fortunate decision, for as soon as the doors cut off the rush of air into the bomb-bay the fire began to subside, although it did not go out completely.

The crew owed their lives to the genius of Barnes Wallis, and the Wellington's revolutionary construction. Another less robust aircraft would probably have broken in half. As it was, the bomber continued to fly, although by the time it crossed the coast and headed out over the English Channel it was losing height steadily. A few minutes later, it became apparent that the bomber would not make landfall, and the pilot decided to put her down in the sea while he still had full control.

The ditching was perfect, and the five-man crew scrambled from the sinking aircraft into their rubber dinghy. They knew that they were not far from the English coast, and when the dawn came they entertained hopes of being picked up quickly. Their ordeal, however, was only just beginning. For fifty-seven hours the dinghy drifted through the freezing waters of the Channel, hidden in fog. In the end it was washed ashore on the Isle of Wight, the five airmen more dead than alive and suffering from exposure. All of them subsequently made a full recovery.

They were the lucky ones. Beginning at 6 a.m. on 8 November, one distress signal after another reached the RAF bomber bases, pathetic messages tapped out in faint Morse Code from bombers crossing the enemy coast on the homeward run. The messages were tragically similar. 'We are running out of fuel... unable to maintain height... ditching in five minutes.' And then silence.

In the grim, grey light of the fog-shrouded dawn of 8 November, Bomber Command began to count the cost. It was high; in fact, it was the Command's heaviest loss so far in a single night. Altogether, thirty-seven aircraft had failed to return, and the stark, tragic fact was that only a handful of them had been the victims of enemy action. At least twenty-five of the missing bombers had run out of petrol, gliding down through the cloud and inky darkness to be lost without trace in the icy waters of the North Sea. A few – very few – struggled over the English coast with their last drop of fuel only to be destroyed in crash-landings.

Twenty-one of the bombers which had taken part in the Berlin raid had not come back, and seven more were missing from the mission to Mannheim. There was reason to believe that almost all of them had been lost when their fuel ran out, for the crews who got back from both targets reported that there had been no sign of enemy night-fighters, and that in most cases anti-aircraft opposition had been surprisingly light. Only thirteen out of the entire force of over two hundred bombers had sustained no more than slight damage from shell splinters; the most seriously hit of all appeared to be the 102 Squadron Wellington which was forced to ditch.

The elderly Whitley bombers of No. 4 Group had suffered the most serious loss; fifty-four had gone out and ten of them – twenty-one per cent

– had not come back. Of the 161 Wellingtons of Nos 1 and 3 Groups which had set out, nineteen failed to return.

Tragically, Air Vice-Marshal Slessor's Hampdens, despatched to targets which were believed to be relatively safe, had taken a bad mauling. A total of nineteen had been sent out, and fourteen had returned. Three of the missing Hampdens had been shot down by an intense flak barrage over Oslo, and the other two had gone down over the Ruhr.

The following evening, BBC announcer Joseph MacLeod, his voice grim, gave the nation the first details of the disastrous raid over the nine o'clock news bulletin. 'Reports are now available from our aircrews,' he said, 'on last night's freak weather which interfered with the biggest offensive our bombers have yet launched against Germany. It was not only phenomenal weather, it was unexpected.'

The last statement was simply not true. The bad weather had been expected, and the Bomber Command planning staff had been well aware of it. Yet the raid had gone ahead, and in its wake came a pathetic confusion of accusation and counteraccusation. The C.-in-C. Bomber Command, Air Marshal Sir Richard Peirse, was criticized by the

Chief of Air Staff, Sir Charles Portal, for allowing the raid to proceed. Peirse in turn blamed inadequate weather forecasting and aircrew inexperience, allegations which were bitterly attacked by Sir Wilfrid Freeman, Portal's deputy. From some quarters there came strong pressure for an immediate enquiry, but this proposal was quietly forgotten in case its findings might have an adverse effect on the morale of Sir Richard Peirse's subordinate commanders. Even the Prime Minister, Winston Churchill, was not given full details of the raid until the following January.

The disaster of the night of 7–8 November had formed an unhappy climax to a year that had seen Bomber Command's losses climb steadily in return for very little significant damage inflicted on the enemy. It spotlighted the urgent need for the re-equipment of the Command with all possible speed, and 1942 would see the phasing out of the old Whitleys and Hampdens and the creation of a formidable night striking force based on four-engined heavy bombers: the Stirling, Halifax and the new Avro Lancaster.

But in the meantime, events had unfolded which would ultimately bring a new dimension to the strategic bombing war. On 7 December 1941, a month to the day after the raid that ran out of fuel, the Japanese attacked Pearl Harbor.

Chapter 7

Target Tokyo

From a distance there seemed to be nothing unusual about the small group of warships plunging through the waters of the Pacific seven hundred miles east of Japan. It was a fairly typical US Navy task force, with two aircraft carriers screened by their watchful escort of cruisers and destroyers.

Close to, however, it became apparent that there was something very unusual about one of the carriers – or, more accurately, about the aircraft ranged on her flight deck. These were no Navy machines, but something much larger and more powerful: North American B-25 Mitchell bombers of the Army Air Force.

The date was 18 April 1942. The carrier was the USS *Hornet*; she formed part of Task Force 16 under the command of Vice-Admiral W. F. Halsey. And in just a few hours' time, she would launch her B-25s on one of the most audacious bombing missions in the history of air warfare: the first-ever air strike on Tokyo.

The weeks that followed the devastating attack on Pearl Harbor had seen the western Allies suffer one reverse after another at the hands of the advancing Japanese. Malaya, Hong Kong and Singapore had fallen; gallant rearguard actions were being fought against hopeless odds in the Netherlands East Indies and the Philippines; and in Burma, Allied forces had begun the long retreat towards the Indian frontier.

This appalling succession of disasters produced a numbing shock effect on the morale of the western powers. The Dutch had seen their homeland overrun in May 1940; now their vital colonies were gone, too. The British, reeling under the onslaught of Germany's U-boats at sea and Rommel's Afrika Korps in the Western Desert, now underwent the agony of seeing their 'impregnable' fortress of Singapore topple like a ripe plum, with almost ridiculous ease, into the hands of imperial Japan.

But it was America, once the shock of Pearl Harbor had given way to a rising tide of anger and determination, who took the initiative in forming a plan that was to give the Allied peoples, military and civilian alike, a much needed shot in the arm at a time when morale had plunged almost to rock bottom. It was a plan which, in its execution, would rock the Japanese nation to its foundations, and would have far greater repercussions and influence on the course of the war than its authors ever dreamed.

The plan was conceived initially in a small way early in January 1942 by Captain Francis Low, an officer on the staff of US Navy Commander-in-Chief Admiral Ernest King. He had been to inspect work on the new attack carrier USS *Hornet*, commissioned the previous October and now about to receive the first of her air squadrons at Norfolk, and had watched with interest as the Navy pilots practised deck landings and take-offs on a 500-foot strip marked out on the airfield adjacent to the shipyard.

Low had been wondering for some time about the possibilities of carrying out an air strike on Japan. To use ordinary carrier aircraft would be out of the question; their range was not long enough, and any task force would have to sail almost to within sight of the enemy coast before launching an attack. But suppose, thought Low, that the Army had a bomber with sufficient range, and the ability to take off in five hundred feet with a load of fuel and bombs on board – then why not put a few of them on a carrier like the *Hornet* and hit targets on the Japanese mainland?

He put the idea to Admiral King, who instructed him to discuss it with the air officer on his staff, Captain Donald Duncan, and present a full report on its feasibility. Duncan was enthusiastic, and immediately started to work out some facts and figures. An experienced pilot, he quickly realized that only one aircraft type might be suitable: the B-25 Mitchell medium bomber. Powered by two 1,700-hp Wright Cyclone engines, the first B-25 had flown in August 1940, the design having been ordered straight 'off the drawing-board' in September 1939. The latest version, the B-25B, was well armed with machine-guns in dorsal, ventral and tail turrets, and could carry up to 3,000 lbs of bombs over a range of 1,300 miles. Its top speed was 300 mph at 15,000 feet, and it carried a crew of five. However, the B-25B needed at least 1,250 feet of runway to take off safely with a 2,000-lb bomb load; whether it could be made light enough to take off in only five hundred feet remained to be seen.

Inside a week, Duncan's feasibility study – fifty pages of it – was on Admiral King's desk. King read through it and at once telephoned General Henry Arnold, the Army Air Force C.-in-C., to arrange a meeting. 'Hap' Arnold had become one of the first American military pilots back in 1911 and had always fought hard, sometimes at the risk of his career, to make the United States a strong air power. He was greatly impressed by the scheme, and agreed to send three B-25s to Norfolk so that their take-off characteristics could be tested under various load configurations.

During the next few days, it was found to everyone's amazement that a stripped-down lightly loaded B-25 could actually take off well within the five hundred feet that represented a carrier's deck length. Captain Duncan had already recommended that the USS *Hornet*, commanded by the able and talented Captain Marc Mitscher, should be the carrier used in the operation, and one day late in January she put to sea with a single B-25 on board. Thirty miles offshore, with the carrier steaming into wind, the B-25 pilot took his bomber roaring down the flight deck, lifted her into the air with 150 feet to spare, and flew back to Norfolk.

Meanwhile, General Arnold had been giving a great deal of thought to the man he would select to organize and lead the operation. He needed a man with tremendous organizational ability; a man who was a highly experienced pilot; and one, moreover, who had the engineering expertise necessary to supervise the technical modifications that would have to be made to the B-25s.

One man, among all the potential candidates, met every requirement admirably. His name was Lieutenant-Colonel James H. Doolittle, one of the leading pioneers of American aviation. He had learned to fly with the US Army in 1918, and in the years after the First World War his flying career had been marked by a number of notable 'firsts'. He had become the first man to span the American continent with a flight from Florida to California; the first American to pilot an aircraft solely by instruments from take-off to landing; the first American to fly an outside loop; and in 1925 he had won the coveted Schneider Trophy for the United States. He had also been a test pilot for the Army Air Corps, had demonstrated American fighter designs overseas, and – of vital importance to this new assignment – he had obtained the degree of a Doctor of Science in aeronautical engineering at the Massachusetts Institute of Technology.

Jimmy Doolittle had recently retired from Shell – in whose service, incidentally, he had played a leading part in persuading the Army Air Corps to use 100-octane fuel, which greatly increased aero-engine performance – when he was recalled to military service in 1940. He was forty-five years old, at the peak of his aviation career (he had been named president of the Institute of Aeronautical Science some months earlier), and yet he welcomed the chance to get back into uniform. During those months of 1940 and 1941, he sensed that America would soon be in the war, and he wanted to play his part.

During 1941 General Arnold, who was an old friend, used him as a kind of trouble-shooter to deal with the hundreds of problems that arose as the US aircraft industry strove to gear up its resources to meet the growing demand for modern aircraft by the armed forces. This was still his job when Arnold summoned him to Washington and gave him first details of the daring scheme to bomb Japan.

Like Captain Duncan, Doolittle realized at once that the B-25 was the only suitable aircraft. The problem was to strip it down so that it could take off from the carrier with a sizeable load of fuel and bombs, while not impairing its performance in any way. He made a lot of calculations, which he submitted to Arnold, and the C.-in-C. told him to get on with the job of modifying the bombers and training their crews while Duncan set up the whole operation and arranged full co-operation between Navy and Air Force – not the easiest of tasks at the best of times.

While Duncan set off for Pearl Harbor to brief Admiral Nimitz, C.-in-C. United States Pacific Fleet, who would be responsible for getting a task force together, Doolittle assembled a team of engineers and took a B-25 apart. He removed the ventral gun turret and installed a rubber 60-gallon fuel tank in its place, and another rubber tank holding 160 gallons was fitted into the catwalk above the bomb-bay. Together with the existing fuel tanks, that made a total of 1,050 gallons. He also removed the top-secret Norden bombsight and replaced it with much cheaper and more rudimentary equipment; the attack was going to be made from low level, and Doolittle reckoned that the sophistication of the Norden would not be necessary. Quite apart from that, no one wanted the new sights to fall into enemy hands. New propellers and de-icing equipment were also fitted, while every weighty item – including radios – that was not thought to be absolutely vital was removed.

After ten days of modifications and trials, Doolittle found himself able to lift a stripped-down B-25 from a 400-foot length of runway while carrying 2,000 lbs of bombs and a full fuel load. While modifications to more B-25s went ahead, General Arnold authorized Doolittle to select his crews, and advised him to draw them from the Air Force's most experienced B-25 units: the 17th Bomb Group and the 89th Reconnaissance Squadron, both of them based on Columbia AFB, South Carolina.

Doolittle flew to Columbia early in February and selected twenty-four crews, all of them volunteers. A week later they reported to Eglin Field, near Pensacola in Florida, where they began intensive training with the modified B-25s. They still had not been told the nature of the target, but by this time some of them were making intelligent guesses. Time and again, Doolittle stressed the need for secrecy; the success of the mission, and their lives, depended on it.

While training continued, the naval task force was taking shape. It was to consist of the carriers *Hornet* and *Enterprise*, two heavy cruisers, two light cruisers, eight destroyers and two tankers, and it was to be commanded by Vice-Admiral W. F. 'Bull' Halsey. He flew to San Francisco, where he met Doolittle and went over the details of the plan. He was able to clear up one thing that had been bothering Doolittle: whether they would have to push their aircraft unceremoniously over the side if they were attacked, leaving room for the Hornet's air squadrons to come on deck and go into action, or whether they would have time to fly off. Halsey told him that they would probably be able to take off and fly to Midway Island if the attack came outside Japanese waters; after that, with Midway out of range, they could either shove their B-25s overboard or take off for Japan, with the prospect of ditching in the China Sea after the raid. If all went well, the *Hornet* would take them as close as possible – but not within four hundred miles

– of the Japanese coast, giving them a sufficient fuel margin to reach China after the attack.

By the middle of March, Doolittle's crews had completed their training, achieving astonishing standards of skill. One pilot even succeeded in taking off after a run of only 287 feet. They now flew down to McClelland Field near Sacramento, California, where the final maintenance checks were to be made. Afterwards, they took their bombers to Alameda Naval Station, near San Francisco, where they finally rendezvoused with their carrier.

Doolittle had decided to take sixteen B-25s on the *Hornet*, and getting them on board was a complex business. Carrier air groups normally fly on when their ships are at sea, but there could be no question of this with the B-25s. They had to be lifted aboard with cranes, and then lashed to the flight deck. They did not have folding wings, like naval aircraft, which ruled out any possibility of their being stowed in the big hangar below decks. When the bombers were all on board the *Hornet* had a distinct stern-heavy appearance, as though a cluster of huge parasites had suddenly descended on that part of her.

The *Hornet* sailed from Alameda on 2 April. Not until she had been at sea for twenty-four hours did Doolittle brief the crews who had been selected to fly the mission; until now not even his second-in-command, Major Jack Hilger of the 89th Reconnaissance Squadron, had known the specific nature of the target – or rather targets, for the B-25s were to hit Yokohama, Osaka, Kobe and Nagoya as well as Toyko. Every day, during the remainder of the voyage, the pilots spent long hours poring over the bulky target intelligence folders which Doolittle, Low and Duncan had assembled. Before long the layout of their objectives, together with the nature of the terrain they would have to fly over to reach them, was as familiar as the cockpits of their bombers.

The *Hornet* rendezvoused with the other warships of Task Force 16 north of the Hawaiian Islands, and sailed straight on across the Pacific towards the launching-point. At dawn on 18 April, the day fixed for the strike, the vessels were still seven hundred miles off the Japanese coast, and the weather was worsening, with a high sea running and the wind strength increasing all the time. Adding to all the other worries, a small Japanese ship was sighted at 6:30 a.m., and although the cruiser *Northampton* was quickly sent off to blow her out of the water, it was certain that if she carried radio she would have had ample time to signal the task force's presence.

Doolittle's original plan had been to take off some time ahead of the others and drop four clusters of incendiary bombs on Tokyo just before nightfall, starting a blaze that would lead the following B-25s straight to the target. Now, because of that one encounter with the Japanese steamer, everything had to be changed. With the possibility that Japanese bombers were even now preparing to take off and attack the task force, Admiral Halsey could not afford to endanger his ships by holding course until they reached the planned launch-point, three hundred miles further on. The take-off would have to be brought forward several hours – and the pilots knew what that meant. Even with full tanks, the bombers might not have enough fuel to reach China.

Then Jimmy Doolittle hit on a scheme that would help alleviate the fuel problem. He ordered ten five-gallon drums of petrol to be loaded on each aircraft, and told the crew chiefs to use them to top up the ventral fuel tank as its level dropped during the flight. Immediately afterwards, Doolittle summoned all the pilots to a last-minute briefing, in which he emphasized take-off procedure. The *Hornet* was battling her way into the teeth of a 35-mph gale and she was pitching violently, so it was vital that the pilots started their take-off run at exactly the right moment, otherwise they would find themselves taking off uphill or diving into the sea.

The crews filed out to their aircraft and climbed aboard. All eyes were on Doolittle's B-25 as its pilot opened the throttle slowly, holding the bomber against the brakes. The bow of the carrier dipped sharply, then began to rise, and at that moment Doolittle released his brakes and gave his engines full power. The B-25 began to move, slowly at first, then gathering speed. With a hundred feet to spare Doolittle lifted her cleanly away from the deck and took her up in a steep climb, turning and bringing her round in a tight circle, flying over the length of the carrier before setting course. There was a reason for this; the bombers' compasses had been affected by the metal mass of the carrier, so by flying over her while Captain Mitscher held her on a westerly heading the pilots could check the accuracy of their instruments.

All sixteen B-25s took off safely, despite the heaving motion of the carrier, and followed Doolittle's bomber in the direction of Japan. The second B-25 to take off, flown by Lieutenant Travis Hoover, formed up with Doolittle and the two machines flew on together. They had 670 miles to go to Tokyo, and for the next four and a half hours there was little to do but hold a steady course, flying at the slowest possible economical cruising speed in order to conserve fuel. Doolittle took turns at sharing the controls with his co-pilot, Lieutenant Richard Cole. The other members of his crew were the navigator, Lieutenant Henry Potter, the bombardier, Sergeant Fred Braemer, and the crew chief, Sergeant Paul. J. Leonard, who also doubled up as gunner.

They stayed low, as low as two hundred feet above the sea. Although the Japanese air defences were not thought to have the benefit of radar, the lower the bombers remained, the less the risk of detection by surface vessels or patrol aircraft.

At 1:30 p.m., Jimmy Doolittle sighted the enemy coast. Potter told him that they would make landfall thirty miles north of Tokyo, and he turned out to be dead right. As they crossed the coast, Doolittle picked out a large lake over on the left, and a quick check with the map confirmed his navigator's accuracy. He turned south, skimming low over a patchwork of fields. Peasants looked up and waved, mistaking the speeding B-25 for one of their own aircraft. Once, Doolittle looked up and saw five Japanese fighters, cruising a couple of thousand feet above, but they made no move to attack and eventually turned away. Another good point about this low-level work was that the B-25's drab camouflage blended in nicely with the background, making the bombers extremely difficult to spot from aircraft flying at a higher altitude.

The bombers thundered on, skirting the slopes of hills, leapfrogging high tension cables. There was no flak; it was just like one of the many training flights back home. Suddenly, dead ahead, was the great sprawling complex of the Japanese capital city, and Doolittle took the B-25 up to 1,500 feet. In the glazed nose, bombardier Fred Braemer peered ahead, searching for the munitions factory that was their target. He found it and steered Doolittle towards it, the pilot holding the aircraft rock-steady in response to the bombardier's instructions. On Doolittle's instrument panel a red light blinked four times, each blink denoting the release of an incendiary cluster. The B-25 jumped, lightened of its 2,000-lb load, and Doolittle opened the throttles, anxious to get clear of the target area.

The flight across Tokyo lasted five minutes. Not until they were over the outer suburbs did flak burst across the sky, far in their wake. There was no time to observe the results of their attack: it was full throttle all the way to the coast, their ground speed aided by a 25-mph tail wind.

Behind Doolittle, the fifteen other B-25s were attacking their assigned targets. Travis Hoover released his bombs and fled, following much the same route as Doolittle, while at Yokosuka Lieutenant Edgar E. McElroy, who had been the thirteenth pilot to take off, had an extraordinary stroke of luck. His target was the docks area, and right in the middle of it was a Ryuho-class aircraft carrier. McElroy dropped a 500-lb bomb slap on the flight deck, causing damage that put the ship out of action for several weeks. He and his crew got away safely.

Other crews were not so lucky. Lieutenant William G. Farrow hit oil storage tanks and an aircraft factory in the Osaka-Kobe area, got away unscathed, flew to China and baled out with the rest of his crew in bad weather, only to be captured by pro-Japanese Chinese and turned over to the enemy. He and another crew member, Corporal C. Spatz, were executed; the other three spent the rest of the war in prison camps.

The B-25 flown by Lieutenant Dean Hallmark also reached China and the crew baled out over Poyang Lake. Two crew members, Sergeant William Deiter and Corporal Donald Fitzmorris, landed in the lake and were drowned; Dean Hallmark was captured and executed; his co-pilot, Lieutenant Robert Meder, died of starvation in prison camp. The sole survivor of Hallmark's crew was the navigator, Lieutenant Chase Neilson, who spent forty months as a prisoner of war.

Some crews had lucky escapes. Lieutenant Richard O. Joyce, the pilot of the sixteenth B-25, was attacked by nine Zero fighters over Tokyo. Their fire ripped a great gash in the bomber's rear fuselage and fragments peppered the tail, but despite this Joyce succeeded in getting away and baled out with his men over friendly Chinese territory. Another pilot, Ross Greening, was also attacked by fighters; his gunner, Sergeant Melville Gardner, shot down one of them and Greening got away. He and his crew also baled out over China, suffering only minor injuries on landing.

The plan was for all the B-25s to head south-west across the China Sea, skirting the Japanese islands of Shikoku and Kyushu, and fly to the Chinese airfield of Chuchow in Chekiang province.

The plan, however, was badly disrupted by the weather. First of all, as Jimmy Doolittle found during the sea crossing, the wind veered, reducing the bombers' ground speed and using up more precious fuel; and then, when they crossed the Chinese coast, they found a thick blanket of cloud stretching as far as the eye could see. Doolittle had been promised that a homing beacon would have been set up at Chuchow, but they could detect no welcoming radio signal from it. In fact, the aircraft carrying it to the field had crashed in the mountains, and it later transpired that the message alerting the Chinese to expect the American bombers had somehow gone astray, so that no one knew they were coming.

Not daring to risk a descent through the murk — there were mountains all around Chuchow, and by this time it was dark – Doolittle ordered his crew to bale out. They were picked up by Chinese troops and eventually arrived at Chuchow to find five crews already there: Major Jack Hilger and Lieutenants Ross Greening, David Jones, William Bower and Robert Gray. Baling out like Doolittle, they had sustained one casualty; Gray's gunner, Corporal Leland D. Faktor, who had been killed when he fractured his skull on landing.

Considering that Chuchow was surrounded on three sides by Japanese forces, it seemed incredible that only two crews, Farrow's and Hallmark's, had actually had the misfortune to land in enemy territory. In the twenty-four hours after the raid, reports began to trickle in about the fate of the others. Captain David Jones, Lieutenant Everett Holstrom and their crews were all safe; Lieutenant Ted Lawson had ditched off the coast despite a badly injured leg and he and his men had struggled ashore, where they were sheltered by Chinese guerrillas. Lawson, however, lost his leg. Lieutenant Harold F. Watson and his crew had baled out about 100 miles south of Poyang Lake; Watson had suffered a broken arm, but no one else was injured. Lieutenant Donald Smith had landed not far from Lawson, and it was one of his crew – Lieutenant T. R. White, the only medical officer on the flight – who had amputated the injured pilot's leg under appallingly primitive conditions.

That left only Captain Edward J. York unaccounted for, and it was some time before Doolittle learned what had become of him. After bombing Tokyo and heading out to sea, York had discovered that his B-25 had used up far more fuel than should have been the case, and there was no possibility of reaching China. He had therefore turned north and landed on Russian territory forty miles north of Vladivostok. He and his crew were interned, and it was only after more than a year of protracted negotiations that the Russians released them.

Of the eighty men who took part in the raid, ten died and fifteen more were injured, in most cases only slightly. Sadly, twelve of Doolittle's gallant band were to die later in the war. Doolittle himself was promoted to the rank of brigadier-general immediately after the raid and awarded the Congressional Medal of Honor. All the other survivors received the Distinguished Flying Cross. Doolittle later commanded the United States 12th

Air Force in North Africa and the 8th Air Force in England.

Although most of the targets assigned to the B-25 crews had been hit, the damage caused had been slight, mainly because the aircraft had carried relatively light bomb loads. The effect on the morale of the Japanese, however, flushed and made cocksure by their recent victories, was incalculable. There was also another consequence: one which was to turn the tide of the war in the Pacific.

As a direct result of the Tokyo raid and its impact, Admiral Yamamoto, commander of the Imperial Japanese Navy, launched an ambitious plan to extend the eastern perimeter of the Japanese defences and bring the American Pacific Fleet to battle. The outcome, in June 1942, was the Battle of Midway, when Yamamoto's task forces were effectively shattered. Midway marked the beginning of the end for Japan's dreams of conquest, and set the stage for the long Allied push back across the Pacific. Before that push ended, Japan's cities would know an agony of fire and destruction that their inhabitants would never have dreamed possible, when Jimmy Doolittle and his men hit Tokyo for the first time.

Chapter 8

Mission to Augsburg

On 17 April 1942, the day before Jimmy Doolittle led his bombers to Tokyo, another audacious daylight mission was flown on the other side of the world. The target was the MAN diesel-engine factory at Augsburg, in Bavaria, which was responsible for the production of roughly half Germany's output of U-boat engines. The Augsburg raid, apart from being one of the most daring and heroic ever undertaken by RAF Bomber Command, was notable for two main things: it was the longest low-level penetration ever made during the Second World War, and it was the first daylight mission flown by the Command's new Lancaster bombers in the teeth of strong enemy opposition.

The prototype Avro Lancaster had been delivered to the RAF for operational trials with No. 44 Squadron at Waddington in September

1941. On 24 December it was followed by three production Lancaster Mk 1s, and the nucleus of the RAF's first Lancaster squadron was formed. In January 1942 the new bomber also began to replace the Avro Manchester of No. 97 Squadron at Coningsby – not before time, for in eighteen months of operations those flying death-traps, whose unreliable Rolls-Royce Vulture engines were prone to bursting into flames without warning, had cost the lives of a lot of aircrew. Nevertheless, the Manchester's basic airframe design had been good, and had given birth to the Lancaster.

Four aircraft of No. 44 Squadron carried out the Lancaster's first operation on 3 March 1942, laying mines in the German Bight, and the first night-bombing mission was flown on 10–11 March when two aircraft of the same squadron took part in a raid on Essen. In all, fifty-nine squadrons of Bomber Command were destined to use Lancasters during World War II: this splendid aircraft was to be the sharp edge of the RAF's sword in the air offensive against Germany. Powered by four Rolls-Royce Merlin engines, the Lancaster carried a crew of seven and had a defensive armament of ten .303

Browning machine-guns. It had a top speed of 287 mph at 11,500 feet and could carry a normal bomb load of 14,000 lbs – although later versions could lift the massive 22,000-lb 'Grand Slam' bomb which was used to pulverize 'hard' targets towards the end of the war.

Because of the havoc wrought by Hitler's U-boats, the MAN factories at Augsburg had long been high on the list of priority targets. The problem was that getting there and back involved a round trip of 1,250 miles over enemy territory, and the factories covered a relatively small area. With the navigation and bombing aids available earlier, the chances of a night attack pinpointing and destroying such an objective were very remote, and a daylight precision attack, going on past experience, would be prohibitively costly.

Then the Lancaster came along, and the idea of a deep-penetration precision attack in daylight was resurrected. With its relatively high speed and strong defensive armament, it was possible that a force of Lancasters could get through to Augsburg if they went in at low level, underneath the German warning radar. Also, a Lancaster flying 'on the deck' could not be subjected to attacks from below, its vulnerable spot. A lot would depend, too, on the route to the target, RAF Intelligence had compiled a reasonably accurate picture of the disposition of enemy fighter units in western Europe, which early in 1942 were seriously overstretched. Half the total German fighter force was employed in Russia and another quarter in the Balkans and North Africa; most of the remaining squadrons, apart from those earmarked for the defence of Germany itself, were stationed in the Pas de Calais area and Norway. The danger point was the coast of France; if the Lancasters could slip through a weak spot, perhaps in conjunction with a strong diversionary attack, then the biggest danger, in theory at least, would be behind them.

Although Bomber Command's new chief, Air Marshal Arthur Harris, was generally opposed to small precision raids – being a strong advocate of large-scale 'area' attacks on enemy cities – the situation in the North Atlantic, with its awful daily toll of Allied shipping, compelled him to authorize the Augsburg plan. If it succeeded, it might put a brake for some time on the number of operational U-boats, and at the same time silence some of the critics who clamoured for the RAF to devote more of its resources to hunting them.

The operation was to be carried out by six crews from No. 44 Squadron at Waddington and six from No. 97, now at Woodhall Spa in Lincolnshire, the two most experienced Lancaster units. A seventh crew from each squadron would train with the others, to be held in reserve in case anything went wrong at the last minute.

For three days, starting on 14 April 1942, the two squadrons practised formation flying at low level, making thousand-mile flights around Britain and carrying out simulated attacks on targets in northern Scotland. It was exhausting work, hauling thirty tons of bomber around the sky at this sort of altitude and having to concentrate on not flying into a neighbouring aircraft as well as obstacles on the ground, but the crews were all highly experienced, most of them going through their second tour of operations, and they achieved a high standard of accuracy in the short time available.

Speculation ran high over the nature of the target. To most of the experienced crews, a low-level mission signified an attack on enemy warships, a long, straight run into a nightmare of flak. When they eventually filed into their briefing rooms early on 17 April, and saw the long red ribbon of their track stretching to Augsburg, a stunned silence descended on them. Even an attack on the *Tirpitz* would have been preferable to this.

Almost automatically, they registered the details passed to them by the briefing officers. The six aircraft from each squadron were to fly in two sections of three, each section leaving the rendez-vous point at a predetermined time. The interval between each section would only be a matter of seconds; visual contact had to be maintained so that the sections could lend support to one another in case they were attacked by enemy fighters.

From the departure point, Selsey Bill, the Lancasters were to cross the Channel at low level and make landfall at Dives-sur-Mer, on the French coast. Shortly before this, bombers of No. 2 Group, covered by a massive fighter 'umbrella', were to make a series of diversionary attacks on Luftwaffe airfields in the Pas de Calais, Rouen and Cherbourg areas. The Lancasters' track would take them across enemy territory via Ludwigshafen, where they would cross the Rhine, to the northern tip of the Ammer See, a large lake some twenty miles west of Munich and about the same distance south of Augsburg. By keeping to this route, it was hoped that the enemy would think that Munich was the target. Only when they reached the Ammer See would the bombers sweep sharply northwards for the final run to their true objective.

As they approached the target, the bombers were to spread out so that there was a three-mile gap between each section. Sections would bomb from low level in formation, each Lancaster dropping a salvo of four 1,000-lb bombs. These would be fitted with eleven-second delayed action fuses, giving the bombers time to get clear and exploding well before the next section arrived over the target. Take-off was to be at 3 p.m., which meant that the first Lancasters should reach the target at 8:15, just before dusk. They would therefore have the shelter of darkness by the time they reached the Channel-coast danger areas on the homeward flight.

The Lancasters of No. 44 Squadron would form the first two sections. This unit was known as the 'Rhodesia' Squadron, with good reason: about a quarter of its personnel came from that country. There were also a number of South Africans, and one of them was chosen to lead the mission. He was Squadron Leader John Dering Nettleton, a tall, dark-haired 25-year-old who had already shown himself to be a highly competent commander, rock-steady in an emergency. The war against the U-boat was of special interest to him, for after leaving school in Natal he had spent two years in the Merchant Navy and consequently had a fair idea of the agonies seamen must go through when their ships were torpedoed. He came from a naval background, too; his grandfather had been an admiral in the Royal Navy.

John Nettleton had joined the Royal Air Force in 1938, and in April 1942 he was still completing his first operational tour, having spent much of the war so far as an instructor. It was one of the penalties of being an above-average pilot: such men were often 'creamed off' to teach others.

At three o'clock in the afternoon of 17 April, the quiet Lincolnshire village of Waddington was rudely shaken by the roar of twenty-four Rolls-Royce Merlins as No. 44 Squadron's six Lancasters took off and headed south for Selsey Bill, the promontory of land jutting out into the Channel between Portsmouth and Bognor Regis. Ten miles due east, the six bombers of No. 97 Squadron, led by Squadron Leader Sherwood, were also taking off from Woodhall Spa.

Each section left Selsey Bill right on schedule, the sea blurring under the Lancasters as they sped on. The bombers to left and right of Nettleton were piloted by Flying Officer John Garwell and Warrant Officer Rhodes; the Lancasters in the following section were flown by Flight Lieutenant Sandford, Warrant Officer Crum and Warrant Officer Beckett. The sky was brilliantly clear and the hot afternoon sun beat down through the perspex of cockpits and gun turrets. Before they reached the French coast, most of the crews were flying in shirtsleeves.

As they raced over the French coast the pilots had to ease back their control columns to leapfrog the cliffs, so low were the great bombers. They thundered inland across the picturesque countryside of Normandy, the broad loops of the River Seine glistening in the sunshine away to the left. The bombers would pass to the south of Paris and on to Sens, on the Yonne River, their first major checkpoint. Sens lay about 180 miles from the Channel coast – about an hour's flying time, at the ground speed the Lancasters were making.

If they survived that first hour, if the diversionary raids had drawn off the German fighters, then they would have a good chance of reaching Augsburg.

The bombers were flying over wooded, hilly country near Breteuil when the flak hit them. Lines of tracer from concealed gun positions met the speeding Lancasters, and the ugly black stains of shellbursts dotted the sky around them. Shrapnel ripped into two of the aircraft, but they held their course. The most serious damage was to Warrant Officer Beckett's machine, which had its rear gun turret put out of action.

It was sheer bad luck that drew the German fighters to the Lancasters. Two squadrons of Messerschmitt 109s belonging to JG 2, the 'Richthofen' Geschwader – one of the most experienced and battle-hardened fighter units in the Luftwaffe – were returning to their base at Evreux after sweeping the area to the south of Paris in search of No. 2 Group's diversionary bombers when they passed directly over the Lancasters' track, actually passing between Nettleton's and Sherwood's formations, although at a much higher altitude. Even then, the bombers might have escaped detection if it had not been for a solitary Messerschmitt 109, much lower than the rest, making an approach to land at Evreux with wheels and flaps down.

The German pilot spotted the Lancasters, chasing their black shadows as they drummed over the woods and fields, and immediately whipped up his landing gear, climbing hard and turning in behind Sandford's section. He must have alerted the other fighters, because a few seconds later they came tumbling like an avalanche on the bombers.

The first 109 came streaking in, singling out Warrant Officer Crum's Lancaster for his first firing pass. Bullets tore through the cockpit canopy, showering Crum and his navigator, Rhodesian Alan Dedman, with razor-sharp slivers of perspex. Dedman looked across at the pilot and saw blood streaming down his face, but when he went to help Crum just grinned and waved him away. The Lancaster's own guns hammered, there was a fleeting glimpse of the 109's pale-grey, oil-streaked belly as it flashed overhead, and then it was gone.

The Lancasters closed up into even tighter formation as thirty more Messerschmitts pounced on them like sharks. The sky became filled with smoky lines of tracer as a vicious running fight developed. The Lancaster pilots held their course doggedly; at this height there was no room to take evasive action and they had to rely on the bombers' combined firepower to keep the Germans at bay.

It was the first time that Luftwaffe fighters had encountered Lancasters, and to begin with the enemy pilots showed a certain amount of caution until they got the measure of the new bomber's defences. As soon as they realized that its defensive armament consisted of .303 machine-guns, however, they began to press home their attacks skilfully, coming in from the port quarter and opening fire with their cannon at about seven hundred yards. At four hundred yards, the limit of the .303's effective range, they broke away sharply and climbed to repeat the process.

The Lancasters were raked time after time as they thundered on, their vibrating fuselages a nightmare of noise as cannon shells punched into them and the gunners returned the enemy fire, their pilots drenched with sweat as they dragged the bombers over telegraph wires, steeples and rooftops. In the villages below, people fled to cover as the battle swept a few feet above their heads and shells from their own fighters spattered the walls of houses.

Warrant Officer Beckett was the first to go. A great ball of orange flame ballooned from a wing of his Lancaster as cannon shells hit a fuel tank. Seconds later, the bomber was a mass of fire. Slowly, the nose went down. Spewing burning fragments, the shattered bomber hit a clump of trees and disintegrated.

Warrant Officer Crum's Lancaster, its wings and fuselage ripped and torn, came under attack by three enemy fighters. Both the mid-upper and rear-gunners were wounded, and now the port wing fuel tank burst into flames. The bomber wallowed on, almost out of control. Crum, half-blinded by the blood streaming from his face wounds, fought to hold the wings level and ordered Alan Dedman to jettison the bombs, which had not yet been armed. The thousand-pounders dropped away, and a few moments later Crum managed to put the crippled aircraft down on her belly. The Lancaster tore across a wheatfield and slewed to a stop on the far side. The crew, badly shaken and bruised but otherwise unhurt, broke all records in getting out of the wreck, convinced that it was going to explode in flames. But the fire in the wing went out, so Crum used an axe from the bomber's escape kit to make holes in the fuel tanks and threw a match into the resulting pool of petrol. Within a couple of minutes the aircraft was burning fiercely; there would only be a very charred carcase left for the Luftwaffe experts to examine.

Afterwards, Crum and his crew split up into pairs and set out to walk through occupied France to Bordeaux, where they knew they could make contact with members of the French Resistance. All of them, however, were subsequently rounded up by the Germans and spent the rest of the war as PoWs.

Now only Flight Lieutenant Sandford was left out of the three Lancasters of the second section. Sandford, a quiet music lover who amused his colleagues because he always wore pyjamas under his flying suit for luck, was one of the most popular officers on No. 44 Squadron. Now his luck had run out, and he was fighting desperately for his life. In a bid to escape from a swarm of Messerschmitts, he eased his great bomber down underneath some high-tension cables. But the Lancaster dug a wingtip into the ground, cartwheeled and exploded, killing all the crew.

The enemy fighters now latched on to Warrant Officer Rhodes, flying to the right and some distance behind John Nettleton. Soon, the Lancaster was streaming fire from all four engines. Rhodes must have opened his throttles wide in a last attempt to draw clear, because his aircraft suddenly shot ahead of Nettleton's. Then it went into a steep climb and seemed to hang on its churning propellers for a long moment before flicking sharply over and diving into the ground. There was no chance of survival for any of his crew.

The Lancaster was shot down by another warrant officer, a man named Pohl. Poor Rhodes was the thousandth victim to be claimed since September 1939, by the redoubtable pilots of JG 2 'Richthofen', and a party was held in Pohl's honour at Evreux that night.

There were only two Lancasters left out of the 44 Squadron formation now; those flown by Nettleton and his No. 2, John Garwell. Both aircraft were badly shot up and their fuel tanks were holed, but the self-sealing 'skins' seemed to be preventing leakage on a serious scale. Nevertheless, the fighters were still coming at them like angry hornets, and the life expectancy of both crews was now measured in minutes.

Then the miracle happened. Suddenly, singly or in pairs, the enemy fighters broke off their attacks and turned away. They were probably running out of fuel or ammunition, or both. Whatever the reason, their abrupt disappearance meant that Nettleton and Garwell were spared, at least for the time being. But they still had more than five hundred miles to go before they reached the target. Behind them, and a little way to the south, Squadron Leader Sherwood's 97 Squadron formation had been luckier; they never saw the German fighters, and flew on unmolested.

Flying almost wingtip to wingtip, Nettleton and Garwell swept on in their battle-scarred aircraft. There was no further enemy opposition, and the two pilots were free to concentrate on handling their bombers – a task that grew more difficult when, two hours later, they penetrated the mountainous country of southern Germany and the Lancasters had to fly through turbulent air currents that boiled up from the slopes.

They reached the Ammer See and turned north, rising a few hundred feet to clear some hills and then dropping down once more into the valley on the other side. And there, dead ahead of them under a thin veil of haze, was Augsburg.

As they reached the outskirts of the town, a curtain of flak burst across the sky in their path. Shrapnel pummelled their wings and fuselages but the pilots held their course, following the line of the river to find their target. The models, photographs and drawings they had studied at the briefing had been astonishingly accurate and they had no difficulty in locating their primary objective, a T-shaped shed where the U-boat engines were manufactured.

With bomb-doors open, and light flak hitting the Lancasters all the time, they thundered over the last few hundred yards. Then the bombers jumped as the 8,000 lbs of bombs fell from their bellies. The Lancasters were already over the northern suburbs of Augsburg when the bombs exploded, and the gunners reported seeing fountains of smoke and debris bursting high into the evening sky above the target.

Nettleton and Garwell had battled their way through appalling odds and successfully accomplished their mission, but the flak was still bursting around them and now John Garwell found himself in trouble. A flak shell turned the interior of the fuselage into a roaring inferno and Garwell knew that this, together with the severe damage the bomber had already sustained, might lead to her breaking up at any moment. There was no time to gain height so that the crew could bale out; he had to put her down as quickly as possible. Blinded by the smoke that was now pouring into the cockpit, Garwell eased the Lancaster gently down towards what he hoped was open ground. He was completely unable to see anything; all he could do was try and hold the bomber steady as she sank.

A long, agonizing minute later the Lancaster hit the ground, sending earth flying in all directions as she skidded across a field. Then she slid to a stop, and Garwell, with three other members of his crew, scrambled thankfully out of the raging heat and choking, fuel-fed smoke into the fresh air. Two other crew members were trapped in the burning fuselage and a third, Flight Sergeant R. J. Flux, had been thrown out on impact. He had wrenched open the escape hatch just before the bomber touched down; his action had given the others a few precious extra seconds in which to get clear, but it had cost Flux his life.

Completely alone now, John Nettleton set course north-westwards for home, chasing the setting sun. Darkness fell, and the crew, as the realization of the sacrifice made by their friends descended on them, fell silent. They were utterly weary, and at the age of twenty or so it was hard to believe that they would never again see others like themselves with whom they had shared so much for so long. But they, at least, would be coming back.

As Nettleton turned for home, the leading section of No. 97 Squadron bored in across the hills towards Augsburg. They had to fly through a flak barrage even more intense than the storm that had greeted Nettleton and Garwell; as well as four-barrelled 20-mm Vierling cannon, the Germans were using batteries of 88-mm guns, their barrels depressed to the minimum and their shells doing far more damage to the buildings of Augsburg than to the racing bombers.

All three Lancasters released their loads on the target and thundered on towards safety, their gunners spraying any anti-aircraft position they could see. The bombers were so low that on occasions they dropped below the level of the rooftops, finding some shelter from the murderous flak.

They also made it, all three of them. Then Sherwood's aircraft, probably hit by a large-calibre shell, began to stream white vapour from a fuel tank. A few moments later flames erupted from it and it went down out of control, a mass of fire, to explode just outside the town. Sherwood alone was thrown clear and survived. The other two pilots, Flying Officers Rodley and Hallows, returned safely to base.

The second section consisted of Flight Lieutenant Penman, Flying Officer Deverill and Warrant Officer Mycock. All three pilots saw Sherwood go down as they roared over Augsburg in the gathering dusk. The sky above the town was a mass of vivid light as the enemy gunners hurled every imaginable kind of flak shell into the Lancasters' path. Mycock's aircraft was quickly hit and set on fire but the pilot held doggedly to his course. By the time he reached the target his Lancaster was little more than a plunging sheet of flame, but Mycock held on long enough to release his bombs. Then the

Lancaster exploded, its burning wreckage cascading into the streets.

Deverill's aircraft was also badly hit and its starboard inner engine set on fire, but the crew managed to extinguish it after bombing the target and flew back to base on three engines, accompanied by Penman's Lancaster. Both crews expected to be attacked by night-fighters on the home run, but the flight was completely uneventful. It was just as well, for every gun turret on both Lancasters was jammed.

For his part in leading the Augsburg raid, John Nettleton was awarded the Victoria Cross. He was promoted wing commander, and the following year saw him flying his second tour of operations.

Sadly, death and John Nettleton were destined to keep a long-delayed rendezvous. On the night of 12–13 July 1943, his bomber fell in flames from the night sky over Turin.

Although reconnaissance later showed that the MAN assembly shop had been damaged, the full results of the raid were not known until after the war. It appeared that five of the delayed-action bombs which the Lancaster crews had braved such dangers to place on the factory had failed to explode. The others caused severe damage to two buildings, one a forging shop and the other a machine-tool store, but the machine-tools themselves suffered only light damage. The total effect on production was negligible, especially as the Maschinenfabrik Augsburg-Nürnberg had five other factories building U-boat engines at the time.

The loss of seven Lancasters and forty-nine young men was too high a price to pay, and the RAF would never again send its four-engined bombers on a daylight 'extreme danger' mission of this kind. The low-level tactics had not worked; although the task of the enemy fighters had been made more difficult by the low altitude at which the bombers flew, this had not prevented them from destroying one-third of the attacking force within a very short space of time. Had the fighters not run short of fuel, they might easily have accounted for the entire formation before it was half way to the target.

In the months after Augsburg, it was the Americans who would provide the 'lance' of the Allied bombing offensive with their daylight precision attacks on high-priority targets, a task in which, by 1944, they were to prove extremely efficient, RAF

Bomber Command, on the other hand, would be the bludgeon, its growing strength hammering Germany's industrial cities night after night. And in 1943 one city above all others was to feel the awesome destructive power of that bludgeon: Hamburg.

Chapter 9

Operation Gomorrah: The Battle of Hamburg

Right from the start, it looked like being a big raid. Since 11:30 on that night of 24 July 1943 a plot had been building up steadily in the underground operations rooms of the Luftwaffe's 1st and 2nd Air Divisions at Deelen, in Holland, and Stade, just west of the Elbe estuary. The RAF bomber stream was once again heading for northern Germany, and the scanners of the big 'Freya' search radars on the coast had picked it up while it was still far out over the North Sea. On the radar screens, the bombers left a trace resembling a procession of crawling ants, each one represented by a pinprick of faint luminosity. First came a relatively small group of pinpricks; these were the bombers of the RAF Pathfinder Force, whose task it was to light up tonight's objective with incendiary bombs and target indicators. Then, a few miles further back, strung out in a broad band across the sea, came the main force, on this occasion several hundred strong.

As yet, the Luftwaffe plotters had no way of knowing where the target lay. All they knew was that the bomber stream was following a route that kept it well to the north of latitude 54 degrees, and that it was flying roughly parallel with the line of the Frisian Islands. If the bombers maintained this course, they would make landfall on the west coast of Schleswig-Holstein, but it was impossible to tell whether they would swing south at this point to strike at Bremen, or carry on across the narrow neck of land south of the Danish border and then veer south to hit Berlin. All the controllers could do was 'scramble' their night-fighters, position them over the sea off the north coast of Germany, and hope for the best.

The night-fighters were twin-engined Messerschmitt 110s, equipped with 'Lichtenstein' airborne interception radar. Each night-fighter operated within the confines of a circular zone, the zones overlapping to form a continuous chain extending from the Baltic to Belgium. Acting on the information received from the 'Freya' warning radars, smaller and shorter-range 'Wurzburg' tracking radars would pick up the bombers as they approached German territory; armed with new information on courses, heights and speeds, controllers would then steer the night-fighters towards their targets. The system had worked reasonably well in 1941, when the night-bombers were still coming over in small numbers, but by 1943 the position had changed completely, with large numbers of bombers literally swamping the night-fighter defences. What the Germans really needed was a new technique enabling them to concentrate their night-fighters in sufficient numbers wherever the bomber stream broke through the defences: but in the summer of 1943 the old system, known as 'Himmelbett', was still in operation, presenting the night-fighter crews and their controllers wih an impossible task.

Already, by the spring of 1943, RAF Bomber Command had been largely re-equipped with four-engined Halifax and Lancaster heavy bombers, and extensive use was being made of two radio aids to navigation, target location and bombing known as 'Oboe' and 'H2S'. The former involved two ground stations transmitting pulses to an aircraft, which received them and re-transmitted them. By measuring the time taken for each pulse to go out and return, the distance from the aircraft to the ground stations could be calculated. If the distance of the target from Station A was known, the aircraft could be guided along the arc of a circle whose radius equalled this distance. The bomb-release point was calculated and determined by Station B, which 'instructed' the aircraft to release its load when the objective was reached. Because of the comparatively small size of 'Oboe' equipment, it was installed mainly in the Command's fast, twin-engined Mosquito bombers.

H2S, which was fitted in Halifaxes and Lancasters, was quite different. This was a form of airborne radar transmitting pulse signals to earth and receiving back the echoes, which formed a display on a cathode-ray tube. The display consisted of a series of dots of varying brilliance, forming a picture of the terrain over which the bomber was flying and enabling the navigator to identify readily-definable features such as coastlines and towns.

Using this equipment, Bomber Command began a major offensive against targets in the Ruhr, Germany's industrial centre, in March 1943. Between 5 March and the end of May Essen, home of the Krupp steel factories, was attacked five times on a massive scale, and so was Duisburg, the target being marked by 'Oboe'-equipped Mosquitoes in each instance. The results were far higher than any achieved previously, and this opening phase of the Battle of the Ruhr marked a significantly important turning-point in the Allied strategic air offensive. It included, incidentally, one of the most spectacular bombing missions of all time – the famous precision attack on the Moehne, Eder and Sorpe Dams by Lancasters of No. 617 Squadron, specially modified to carry a 9,250-lb cylindrical mine developed by the indefatigable Barnes Wallis. The Moehne and Eder Dams were successfully breached, causing considerable devastation through flooding, but out of the seventeen Lancasters that made the attack eight failed to return. The leader of the mission, Wing Commander Guy Gibson, was awarded the Victoria Cross.

Although the dam raid achieved enormous publicity and captured the imagination of the British public, there was no escaping the fact that it had achieved only partial success, and at very high cost. Fifty-six men – about half 617 Squadron's highly trained aircrew – had not come back. It served to strengthen the view of Air Marshal Harris that concentrated 'area' attacks on Germany's industrial cities by large numbers of night-bombers provided the real means of hurting the enemy, at the same time keeping Bomber Command's loss rate down to an acceptable level.

During the first half of 1943, however, there was a problem. Although the key to good bombing results seemed to lie in accurate and effective target marking techniques, which were now possible with the use of 'Oboe', it was a different story when Bomber Command struck at targets deeper in Germany, which were out of range of the home-based 'Oboe' stations. An attack on Munich early in March caused only light damage, while another on Stuttgart failed almost completely. Towards the end of the month two raids were made on Berlin, and out of nearly five hundred aircraft that took part only three dropped their bombs anywhere near the aiming-point. The same sort of negative result occurred on other raids on Kiel, Frankfurt and Stuttgart.

A number of factors added up to these failures, not the least of which was that the timing of the main bomber stream left a lot to be desired. Many aircraft arrived over the target well behind schedule to find that target indicators, carefully placed by the Pathfinder Force, had gone out. The main limitation, however, was H2S, which was used as the principal navigation aid in pinpointing all long-range targets in 1943. Often, accurate interpretation of H2S was extremely difficult unless the target was adjacent to some prominent terrain feature such as a river or coastline. Identification, moreover, became more difficult the higher a bomber flew, and the Lancasters and Halifaxes often had to fly close to their maximum ceilings to escape bad weather or heavy enemy defences.

'Bomber' Harris knew that during the attacks on the Ruhr in the spring and early summer of 1943, his Command had hurt the enemy as never before. What he needed now was to achieve even better results against a target which was further afield; one which could be located accurately by H2S, marked accurately by the pathfinders, and afterwards subjected to the greatest bombing concentration in the history of air warfare.

The choice of target seemed obvious. It was Hamburg, the second largest city in Germany and the second largest seaport in the world. Sprawling on the estuary of the River Elbe, it could be readily identified on H2S, and there was the added advantage that the bombers carrying out the attack would not have to fly for long distances over enemy territory. They could remain well to the north of the German coastline until the last leg of their flight, then follow the Elbe all the way to their target.

The area around the Elbe estuary and Hamburg itself were, admittedly, heavily defended, but Harris had a big trump-card up his sleeve. This was a simple yet highly effective radar countermeasures device code-named 'Window', consisting of thousands of strips of tinfoil corresponding to the wavelengths of the enemy radar frequencies. When dumped in large quantities and at regular intervals from the bombers it produced radar echoes similar to those of an aircraft, presenting the radar controllers with an overwhelming amount of indecipherable 'clutter'.

Although 'Window' had been perfected early in 1942, the decision to use it operationally had been postponed in case the Germans also developed it for use by the Luftwaffe's bomber force. (In fact the enemy already knew all about the principle, which they called 'Laminetta', but had not used it operationally for precisely the same reason.) It was only in March 1943, when it was finally realized that the German bomber arm no longer presented a serious threat to the British Isles, that the situation took a new turn. Bomber Command's losses were increasing all the time, and it was estimated that about seventy per cent of the total casualties were due to enemy night-fighter activity. Since the enemy night-fighters were radar-controlled they were subject to radar jamming, as were a large number of anti-aircraft and searchlight batteries, and consequently the Air Staff estimated that it might be possible to cut down the Command's loss rate by something like thirty-five per cent. Even then, the decision to employ 'Window' was subjected to still more delay, mainly because it was feared that if the Germans began using it on a large scale they might seriously interfere with Allied plans for the invasion of Sicily, due to take place in the summer of 1943. It was not until 15 July 1943 that the British War Cabinet gave the necessary approval for its introduction, and it was to make its operational debut on the night of 24–25 July, the date fixed for the opening of the Battle of Hamburg.

The Hamburg attack was code-named, appropriately, Operation Gomorrah. It was in fact to consist of a series of four raids: the first on 24–25 July, the second and third on 27–28 and 29–30 July, and the last on 2–3 August. Nothing like it had ever been known before. A hundred years earlier, in 1842, the old city had been destroyed by fire; now Harris was determined that it should happen again, his bombers inflicting such destruction on Hamburg and its $1\frac{3}{4}$ million people that the shock-wave would ripple throughout the Third Reich.

The force sent out to Hamburg on the night of 24 July numbered 791 bombers, consisting of 347 Lancasters, 246 Halifaxes, 125 Stirlings and 73 Wellingtons. The whole force was briefed to keep well to the north of latitude 54 degrees, turning in to make landfall on the German coast near the Elbe estuary. Ahead of the main force, six aircraft of the Pathfinder Force were to drop yellow markers over the crossing-point on the coast, at the same time transmitting their estimate of the latest wind conditions to a ground station in England for relay to the main force. This information would be particularly useful for the aircraft which were not equipped with H2S, enabling their navigators to revise headings and estimated times. All aircraft in the main force carried 'Window', corresponding to the wavelength of the German 'Wurzburg' gun-laying and night-fighter control radars, which worked on 570 megahertz. It was also hoped that the tin-foil strips would interfere with the night-fighters' 'Lichtenstein' airborne radar.

Such was the massive opposition that confronted the widely-scattered Messerschmitt 110s of the Luftwaffe's 1st and 2nd Air Divisions, cruising at their 'Himmelbett' stations that night. The headphones of their crews crackled with the reports from the radar tracking stations and the observers peered intently at their 'Lichtenstein' scanners, seeking first contact with the enemy.

Fifteen minutes after midnight the head of the bomber stream was at position 54 degrees 10 minutes north, 07 degrees 30 minutes east, placing it some twenty miles west of Heligoland. In just a few more minutes, the 'Wurzburg' controllers would be steering the Messerschmitts to make their first interceptions.

Then the incredible happened. At that precise moment, the bombers started releasing their 'Window' at the rate of one bundle a minute. They would maintain this tempo until they passed 07 degrees east on the homeward journey.

The effect on the German radar was instantaneous and startling. The radar screens, which up to now had been registering the steady oncoming of the bombers, suddenly dissolved into a jumble of luminous blobs and spidery lines. British monitoring stations, listening continuously to enemy radio broadcasts, picked up some frantic calls between the night-fighters and their controlling stations:

'The enemy are reproducing themselves!'

'This is impossible – there are too many hostiles! I cannot follow any of them!'

'My Emil is being interfered with!' (Emil was the German code-name for the radar receiver of the 'Lichtenstein' apparatus).

And so it went on, with the Germans taken completely by surprise by this unexpected turn of events and their radar eyes completely blinded. A few minutes later, the night-fighter crews reported sighting bursts of yellow light over the mouth of the Elbe; these were the flares of the six marker aircraft, indicating the landfall point for the main force.

Forty minutes after midnight, as the bomber stream turned south-east and ground observers reported that it was passing over Meldorf, on the Elbe, there was no longer any doubt as to the target. The British were heading for Hamburg, in great strength. But Hamburg's radar-directed flak batteries and searchlights were blinded, too; all the commanders of the city's eighty flak batteries could do was to point their gun barrels towards the north-west and open fire in the hope that their combined barrage would hit something.

The attack began on schedule, fifty-seven minutes into the morning of 25 July, when twenty Pathfinder Force aircraft, all equipped with H2S, dropped yellow target indicators and flares over Hamburg. Behind them came six more H2S-equipped bombers — the same six which had marked the coastal crossing-point — and with the help of the flares their crews were able to identify the target visually and drop clusters of red markers on the aiming-point in the centre of the city.

It was now 1 a.m. Beginning two minutes later, fifty-three more marker aircraft, which also carried high explosive and incendiary loads, dropped green target indicators on the spot where the red markers still burned brightly. The rest of the main force had been briefed to aim at these green indicators if they were unable to see the reds. The latter, in fact, had been quite widely scattered, but with the help of the green indicators dropped by the fifty-three backup aircraft between 1:02 and 1:48 the leading elements of the main force were able to concentrate their bombing quite well on the dockyards and the city. After that a phenomenon known as 'creepback' started to develop; as fires spread out towards the north-west bomber crews tended to aim at these in an understandable eagerness to get clear of the target area, so that by 1:30 a trail of fire stretched back over seven miles between the docks area of Hamburg and a point well beyond the city's outer limits.

Nevertheless, 306 out of the 728 crews who claimed to have attacked the target dropped their bombs within three miles of the aiming-point, and the damage they caused was appalling. It took the whole great armada of bombers only about fifty minutes to pass through the target area, and in that time they dropped 2,396 tons of bombs on the unfortunate city. A high proportion of the bombs used were incendiaries, and as the flames swept through the shattered streets the fires joined up with each other in a conflagration the city's fire services were powerless to stem. As the flames roared higher, air from the city's perimeter was sucked in towards them, fanning them into still greater intensity. It was the first man-made firestorm in history, and its terrible effect was described in the words of a secret German report on the raid which was found in the archives after the end of the war.

Trees three feet thick were broken off or uprooted, human beings were thrown to the ground or flung alive into the flames by winds which exceeded a hundred and fifty miles an hour.

The panic-stricken citizens did not know where to turn. Flames drove them from the shelters, but high-explosive bombs sent them scurrying back again. Once inside, they were suffocated by carbon-monoxide poisoning and their bodies reduced to ashes as though they had been placed in a crematorium, which was indeed what each shelter proved to be. The fortunate were those who jumped into the canals and waterways and remained swimming or standing up to their necks in water for hours until the heat died down.

Twelve RAF aircraft failed to return from this raid and thirty-one were damaged. In Hamburg 1,500 people were killed.

The next morning, General Ira Eaker's 8th US Army Air Force joined the assault, with groups of the 1st Bomb Wing dispatched to attack shipyards and diesel-engine works in Hamburg by daylight. Crews reported that a pall of smoke 15,000 feet high hung over the city from the previous RAF raid, making it difficult to sight the objectives, and only the leading formation was able to bomb before cloud crept over the target area. The cost was high, with nineteen B-17 Flying Fortresses shot down. Many German fighters were airborne over Hamburg, and the luckless Americans bore the brunt of their vengeful attacks. The Americans also carried out daylight attacks on 26 July, sending out some 230 Fortress and Liberator sorties on both days. After each of these daylight attacks, a small force of RAF Mosquito bombers flew nuisance raids against the city, keeping the defenders and the population in a constant state of nervous tension.

In the second big RAF attack, on the night of 27–28 July, a total of 787 bombers was dispatched. This time, in a bid to lead the Germans to believe that Berlin was the target, the bomber stream flew across the neck of Denmark and then turned in to approach Hamburg from the north-east, over Lübeck Bay. 'Window' was once again used and the target was marked by twenty-five bombers using H2S. They were very accurate, their markers going down between one and a half and three miles east-south-east of the aiming-point. The crews that followed found no difficulty in locating the target, and of the 653 crews who attacked it 325 placed their bombs within three miles of it. There was little creepback and the bombers achieved an impressively high standard of concentration; the city's Billwarder district was almost completely razed to the ground, and when the usual small force of Mosquitoes raided Hamburg twenty-four hours later their crews reported that it was still burning fiercely. Seventeen bombers failed to return and forty-nine were damaged; the loss rate had once again been low, thanks in the main to the use of 'Window'.

It was much higher during the third raid, on the night of 29–30 July, and there was some indication that the radar countermeasures were beginning to lose some of their effectiveness. On this occasion the target marking was not very effective, and of the 699 crews who claimed to have hit the target only 238 placed their bombs within the three-mile radius around the aiming-point. Thirty bombers were shot down and a further forty-three damaged, and the returning crews reported that they were encountering growing numbers of single-engined fighters over Hamburg itself. The Germans, in fact, had revised their night-fighter tactics completely; the Messerschmitt 110s of Nacht-Jagdeschwader 3, which were responsible for the night air defence of Hamburg, now operated much closer to the city so that they could benefit from information on the course, height and speed of the bomber stream passed to their control centres from a network of ground observers. Also, Messerschmitt 109s and Focke-Wulf 190s from day-fighter units in the area would circle high above Hamburg, waiting for a sight of the bombers against the fires below.

Thirty bombers also failed to return from the fourth raid, mounted on the night of 2–3 August by 740 bombers. Crews who reached the target area found it covered by dense cloud up to 15,000 feet, with some cloud tops rising to 30,000 feet; below it, Hamburg was drenched by torrential rain, which aided the fire services considerably during the attack. Only about half the bombers located the target, and hardly any of the markers could be seen.

The damage, however, had already been done. In four missions Bomber Command had dispatched over 3,000 aircraft to the city, dropping nine thousand tons of bombs, half of them incendiaries. Eighty-six bombers had failed to return, an astonishingly low cost compared to the results achieved.

In the charred ruins of Hamburg lay the bodies of 30,482 of its inhabitants. Almost half the city, amounting to some 30,480 buildings, had been reduced to rubble. As Air Chief Marshal Sir Arthur Harris had predicted, the shock to the German people was profound. One man on whom the Hamburg catastrophe made a profound impression was Colonel (later General) Adolf Galland, who for months had been urging the allocation of top priority to German fighter production, and particularly the development of jet fighters, in anticipation of the holocaust that was to come. He wrote:

A wave of terror radiated from the suffering city and spread throughout

Germany. Appalling details of the great fires were recounted, and their glow could be seen for days from a distance of a hundred and twenty miles. A stream of haggard, terrified refugees flowed into the neighbouring provinces. In every large town people said, 'What happened to Hamburg yesterday can happen to us tomorrow.' Berlin was evacuated with signs of panic. In spite of the strictest reticence in the official communiqués, the Terror of Hamburg spread rapidly to the remotest villages of the Reich.

Psychologically the war at that moment had perhaps reached its most critical point. Stalingrad had been worse, but Hamburg was not hundreds of miles away on the Volga, but on the Elbe, right in the heart of Germany. After Hamburg, in the wide circle of the political and the military command could be heard the words: 'The war is lost.'

In his secret diaries, the German Propaganda Minister, Dr Josef Goebbels, also expressed grave misgivings which, if Sir Arthur Harris could have known of them at the time, would probably have made Bomber Command's chief dance for joy:

> Reports from the Rhineland indicate that in some cities people are gradually getting rather weak in the knees. That is understandable. For months the working population has had to go into air-raid shelters night after night, and when they come out again they see part of their city going up in flames and smoke. The enervating thing about it is that we are not in a position to reply in kind to the English. Our war in the east has lost us air supremacy in essential sections of Europe and we are completely at the mercy of the English.

Quite apart from its effect on enemy morale, Operation Gomorrah had a far wider consequence on German war policy than Sir Arthur Harris, or anyone else for that matter, could have foreseen when the raids were conceived. After Hamburg, with the Luftwaffe's senior commanders showing a unity that had never been present before, the German aviation industry was ordered by Hermann Göring to concentrate on the production of fighters and the whole German air-defence system was given a complete shake-up, while Adolf Hitler – obsessed more than ever before with reprisal attacks on British cities – gave new priority to the development of new secret weapons such as the V-1 flying bomb and the V-2 rocket.

The Luftwaffe's commanders, however, knew that only one thing could now save Germany: fighters and still more fighters, new designs or improvements on existing ones, to be used in conjunction with more modern air-defence equipment in such a way that would make Allied air attacks on Germany a prohibitively costly business.

The Allies knew, just as clearly, that Germany's capacity to produce those fighters would have to be destroyed. No one stood to suffer more heavily at the hands of the Luftwaffe than the Americans, with their big daylight bomber formations; and it was the Americans who, a fortnight after the week-long battle of Hamburg drew to its close, struck the first big blow in a new offensive against the enemy's aircraft factories.

Chapter 10

The Anniversary Disaster
17 August 1943

On 17 August 1942 twelve Boeing B-17 Fortresses of the 340th, 342nd and 414th Bombardment Squadrons, 97th Bomb Group, United States Eighth Army Air Force, took off from their base at Grafton Underwood in Northamptonshire and climbed to 23,000 feet over the harvest fields of southern England, flying in two flights of six. The leading aircraft of the first flight carried the commanding general of VIII Bomber Command, Ira C. Eaker, and the co-pilot of the first B-17 in the second flight was a young man whose name would one day be blazoned across the front pages of the world's newspapers. Three years later, in another August mission, Major Paul W. Tibbets would pilot a B-29 Superfortress named *Enola Gay* to Hiroshima, carrying in her belly the most devastating weapon known to mankind.

The twelve Fortresses droned over the English Channel in the afternoon sunshine, escorted by four squadrons of RAF Spitfires. Shortly before five o'clock the American crews sighted their target: the marshalling yards at Rouen. While the Spitfires kept a few Messerschmitt 109s at a respectful distance, the Fortresses unloaded eighteen tons of bombs in the target area and turned for home, all landing safely soon after seven o'clock. So, on an optimistic note, ended the first American bombing mission of World War II over the continent of Europe.

General Eaker's VIII Bomber Command had come a long way in the year since that first brief foray into enemy territory. By January 1943, with five hundred B-17s under his command and his crews having experienced a series of encouraging raids on 'fringe' targets in France and the Low Countries, Eaker had decided that the time had come to attack targets in Germany itself. The first was carried out on 27 January 1943, when fifty-three Fortresses bombed Wilhelmshaven for the loss of three of their number, and during the next six months the Americans penetrated to targets such as Hamm, Bremen, Aschersleben, Kassel and

Hannover. These attacks, although they continued to grow in size, also grew in cost; Thunderbolt and Lightning escort fighters, fitted with auxiliary fuel tanks, could accompany the bombers as far as the German frontier, but after that they were on their own. During an intensive series of operations in the last week of July the Americans lost eighty-eight bombers, mostly Fortresses.

Despite these growing losses, and the increasingly determined and savage assaults of the Luftwaffe fighter squadrons, preparations went ahead for the most ambitious strike so far undertaken by VIII Bomber Command: a concentrated attack on the Messerschmitt aircraft factory at Regensburg, a high-priority target which was responsible for a large proportion of Germany's total fighter production. To confuse the enemy defences, plans were also laid for a simultaneous attack on the ball-bearing factories at Schweinfurt, which were in themselves vital to Germany's war industry.

Regensburg was assigned to the B-17s of the 4th Bomb Wing, seven groups totalling 147 aircraft. Because of the distance involved, the plan called for the Regensburg force to fly on to bases in North Africa after hitting the target, which involved a flight across the Alps. The 4th Wing's B-17s were fitted with new long-range 'Tokyo' fuel tanks, making the lengthy trip across the Mediterranean possible. In that way, they would not have to run through a nightmare of flak and fighters a second time.

The Schweinfurt force – 230 bombers of the 1st Bomb Wing – was not so fortunate. Most of the 1st Wing's B-17s had not yet been fitted with Tokyo tanks, and the existing fuel tankage did not give the Fortresses sufficient range to reach North Africa.

The 1st Wing, therefore, had no alternative but to battle its way back to its East Anglian bases through the hornet's nest it would already have stirred up over Germany and Holland.

The dual raid was scheduled to take place on 17 August 1943, a year to the day after that first mission to Rouen. The crews were stood down on the sixteenth, a fairly sure indication that they would be called upon to operate the following day, weather permitting, and there was a lot of speculation about the nature of the target. The 4th Wing's crews were completely mystified when they were told to pack their eating 'irons', razor and toilet articles, spare underwear and a blanket; it was not until the briefing, held during the early hours of the 17th, that they learned they were to spend the following night on another continent.

Those, that was, who survived. Because when they saw their target, the crews were under no illusion. They could expect a big battle over Germany that day, and many of them would not live to see another sunset.

Take-off was scheduled for dawn. The B-17s stood on their dispersals, monsters shrouded in summer mist, laden with fuel and 5,000 lbs of bombs. The sun rose, but the mist refused to burn away, its grey banks clinging to the flat surfaces of the airfields and rendering visibility too bad for take-off in safety. The Regensburg force could not afford to be delayed more than ninety minutes if the bombers were to reach North Africa before dark, and for a time it looked as though the mission might have to be cancelled. Then, suddenly, the mist began to clear and the 4th Wing was ordered off. More problems followed; because of fairly dense cloud conditions over Norfolk and Suffolk, several groups of bombers had great difficulty in making rendezvous, causing the whole vast B-17 formation to cruise in circles over East Anglia for more than two hours before the joining-up procedure was completed. Finally, at 9:35 a.m., the leading groups turned out over the coast near Lowestoft, setting course for Holland; but the comfortable margin of fuel that had given the crews a measure of security no longer existed. The B-17s still carried enough petrol to take them across the Mediterranean, but there was no room now for any diversion from the planned route. The crews knew that their chances of survival, even if they made it out of enemy territory, depended on the skill of their navigators.

To make matters worse, the 1st Wing's bombers still remained on the ground. Their bases were further inland, where the mist tended to be thicker, and it consequently took much longer to disperse. The main complication was that the four groups of P-47 Thunderbolt fighters earmarked for the mission had all been assigned to escort the 4th Wing, the idea being that they would draw enemy fighters away from the Schweinfurt force, due to make its penetration a short time later than the Regensburg force. The longer the bombers destined for Schweinfurt stayed on the ground, the longer the German fighters would have to refuel and rearm and be ready to meet them when they finally did come. In the end, it was decided to postpone the Schweinfurt attack until the afternoon, by which time the Thunderbolts would have returned from the Regensburg mission. It looked as though the unfortunate fighter pilots were going to have to fly a second lengthy sortie that day.

What was more to the point, however, was that the whole purpose behind the two-pronged attack had been destroyed. Both attacking forces, entering enemy territory with hours between them, would feel the full weight of the enemy defences.

At 10 a.m. the leading bomber groups, flying in formations of twenty-one aircraft, crossed the Dutch coast. Forming the first combat wing were the 96th, 388th and 390th Groups; the 4th Wing's commander, Colonel Curtis Le May, flew in a B-17 of the 96th. Years later, as a general, he would rise to command a striking-force against whose awesome power today's mission was not even so much as a pinprick: the mighty nuclear deterrent of Strategic Air Command.

The next two combat wings were each composed of two groups. First came the 94th under Colonel Frederick Castle and the 385th led by Colonel Elliott Vandevanter; and finally, bringing up the rear, were the 95th and 100th Groups, the latter in the most unenviable position of all. It was almost always the rearmost group that suffered most heavily from the attentions of enemy fighters, and today was to be no exception.

The formation droned on into Holland, each combat wing stepped up like a staircase from 17,000 to 19,000 feet, with one group of P-47s weaving watchfully over the leading elements. A second group of fighters, which should have guarded the rear elements, failed to turn up because of a timing error and left these B-17 groups at the mercy of the enemy fighters.

As the formation passed Woensdrecht, with fifteen miles between the first and the last B-17 groups, the first clusters of flak started to come up. The time was 10:17. By this time the rearmost group had begun to trail quite badly, and it was not long before the German fighters realized the fact and exploited it.

Ever since the Fortresses had passed over the Dutch coast, they had been shadowed by the Focke-Wulf 190 fighters of Jagdgeschwader 1. So far, they had not attacked, because the Luftwaffe 1st Division HQ controllers at Deelen had predicted, quite rightly, that the raid would shortly veer south and head into Germany, and that before long the Thunderbolt escort would have to turn back. Now, however, the German fighter pilots saw that the rear B-17 groups were unprotected, and decided that it was too good a chance to miss. As the American formation swung south-eastward over Belgium, twenty miles from Brussels, the first Focke-Wulfs swept down to the attack.

At 10:25 the Focke-Wulfs came curving down in pairs, making fast head-on attacks on the lowest squadron of the trailing 100th Group, their cannon and machine-guns blazing. The Fortress gunners blazed away at them as they flashed past; the big bombers trembled to the recoil of their .5-inch machine-guns and the pungent, sickly smell of burnt cordite drifted through the narrow fuselages.

The Focke-Wulfs sped through the formation, then climbed hard, turning and arrowing down once more to repeat the process. This time, three B-17s – two from the 100th Group and three from the 95th – began to smoke. They held station for a short time, then gradually dropped out of formation. One of them, completely out of control, turned over on its back and fell into a ponderous spin. A few thousand feet lower down it blew up, burning debris spewing from a spreading black smoke cloud.

It was 10:32. Up ahead, the Thunderbolt group which had been covering the lead elements now turned for home. The pilots could see the black smoke trails where the Fortresses had plunged to earth from the rear groups, and enemy fighters buzzing around the silvery B-17s like hornets, but there was nothing they could do to help. They had stayed as long as they dared, and they had just enough fuel left to get back to base.

Flying as co-pilot and observer in *Piccadilly Lily*, one of the 100th Group's B-17s, was Lieutenant-Colonel Beirne Lay Jr, who had been one of the original team of seven USAAF officers to arrive in England with General Eaker in February 1942. He later gave a graphic account of the bombers' agony during the next ninety minutes, as they droned into Germany over the wooded hillsides of the Eifel.

> The gunners reported fighters coming up from all around the clock, singly and in pairs, both Fw 190s and Me 109s. Every gun from every B-17 in our Group was firing, crisscrossing our patch of sky

with tracers. Both sides got hurt in this clash, with two Fortresses from our low squadron and one from the Group ahead falling out of formation on fire with crews bailing out, and several fighters heading for the deck in flames or with their pilots lingering behind under dirty yellow parachutes. I noticed an Me 110 sitting out of range on our right. He was to stay with us all the way to the target, apparently reporting our position to fresh squadrons waiting for us down the road. At the sight of all these fighters, I had the distinct feeling of being trapped. The life expectancy of our Group suddenly seemed very short, since it appeared that the fighters were passing up the preceding Groups in order to take a cut at us.

Swinging their yellow noses round in a wide U-turn, a twelve-ship squadron of Me 109s came in from twelve to two o'clock in pairs and in fours, and the main event was on.

A shining silver object sailed over our right wing. I recognized it as a main exit door. Seconds later, a dark object came hurtling through the formation, barely missing several props. It was a man, clasping his knees to his head, revolving like a diver in a triple somersault. I didn't see his chute open.

A B-17 gradually turned out of the formation to the right, maintaining altitude. In a split second, the B-17 completely disappeared in a brilliant explosion, from which the only remains were four small balls of fire, the fuel tanks, which were quickly consumed as they fell earthward.

Our airplane was endangered by falling debris. Emergency hatches, exit doors, prematurely opened parachutes, bodies, and assorted fragments of B-17s and Hun fighters breezed past us in the slip-stream. I watched two fighters explode not far beneath, disappearing in sheets of orange flame, B-17s dropping out in every state of distress, from engines on fire to control surfaces shot away, friendly and enemy parachutes floating down, and, on the green carpet far behind us, numerous pyres of smoke from fallen fighters, marking our trail. The sight was fantastic; it surpassed fiction.

On we flew through the strewn wake of a desperate air battle, where disintegrating aircraft were commonplace and sixty chutes in the air at one time were hardly worth a second look. I watched a B-17 turn slowly to the right with its cockpit a mass of flames. The co-pilot crawled out of his window, held on with one hand, reached back for his chute, buckled it on, let go and was whisked back into the horizontal stabilizer. I believe the impact killed him. His chute didn't open.

Ten minutes, twenty minutes, thirty minutes, and still no letup in the attacks. The fighters queued up like a breadline and let us have it. Each second of time had a cannon shell in it. Our B-17 shook steadily with the fire of its .50s, and the air inside was heavy with smoke. It was cold in the cockpit, but when I looked across at the pilot I saw that sweat was pouring off his forehead and over his oxygen mask. He turned the controls over to me for a while. It was a blessed relief to concentrate on holding station in formation instead of watching those everlasting fighters boring in. It was possible to forget the fighters. Then the top turret gunner's twin muzzles would pound away a foot above my head, giving a realistic imitation of cannon shells exploding in the cockpit, while I gave an even better imitation of a man jumping six inches out of his seat.

A B-17 of the Group ahead, with its right Tokyo tanks on fire, dropped back to about two hundred feet above our right wing and stayed there while seven of the crew successively bailed out. Four went out the bomb-bay and executed delayed jumps, one bailed from the nose, opened his chute prematurely, and nearly fouled the tail. Another went out the left waist-gun opening, delaying his chute opening for a safe interval. The tail gunner dropped out of his hatch, apparently pulling the ripcord before he was clear of the ship. His chute opened instantly, barely missing the tail, and jerked him so hard that both his shoes came off. He hung limp in his harness, whereas the others had shown immediate signs of life after their chutes opened, shifting around in the harness. The B-17 then dropped back in a medium spiral and I did not see the pilots leave. I saw it just before it passed from view, several thousand feet below us, with its right wing a sheet of yellow flame.

After we had been under constant attack for a solid hour, it appeared certain that our Group was faced with annihilation. Seven of us had been shot down, the sky was still mottled with rising fighters, and it was still only 1120 hours, with target-time still thirty-five minutes away. I doubt if a man in the Group visualized the possibility of our getting much further without one hundred per cent loss. I know that I had long since mentally accepted the fact of death, and that it was simply a question of the next second or the next minute. I learned firsthand that a man can resign himself to the certainty of death without becoming panicky. Our Group fire power was reduced thirty-three per cent; ammunition was running low. Our tail guns had to be replenished from another gun station. Gunners were becoming exhausted.

By this time, most of the single-engined Focke-Wulfs and Messerschmitts had dropped out of the fight, returning to their bases to rearm and refuel. Their place, however, was taken by twin-engined Messerschmitt 110s and Junkers 88s, which – still concentrating on the unfortunate rear groups – attacked with cannon and air-to-air rockets.

Then, as the bombers approached their initial point – the point where they turned for the final run towards the target – at 11:50, the fighter attacks suddenly eased off after a non-stop ninety-minute onslaught. The 100th Group now had fourteen B-17s left out of its original twenty-one, and most of the survivors were damaged, two of them seriously.

Curtis Le May and the pilots of the leading combat wing had no difficulty in picking out the

Messerschmitt factory, nestling in a bend of the River Danube. Visibility was perfect, flak was negligible and the bombing concentration achieved by all groups was excellent. 'As we turned and headed for the Alps,' Col. Lay reported, 'I got a grim satisfaction out of seeing a rectangular column of smoke rising straight up from the Me 109 shops.'

The damage in fact had been extensive, and although Allied Intelligence was unaware of it at the time there had been an unexpected bonus; the bombs had destroyed most of the fuselage jigs for the Messerschmitt 262, the new and highly secret jet fighter with which the Germans hoped to establish total air superiority over western Europe. Production was set back several months, and by the time it recovered Hitler had intervened in the Me 262 programme, ordering the jets to be converted into 'reprisal bombers' and therefore destroying any chance of their use as fighters on a large enough scale in time to turn the course of the air war.

Le May led his bombers over the Alps and down into Italy, descending to an altitude more suitable for economical cruise. Nevertheless, five more B-17s ran out of fuel and had to ditch in the Mediterranean, another made a forced landing in northern

Italy, and two more crash-landed in Switzerland. One of them was one of the badly damaged 100th Group aircraft. Total losses were twenty-four B-17s, fourteen of them from the rear combat wing and ten from the 100th Group – fifty per cent of its aircraft.

The surviving B-17s were widely scattered by the time they reached the Tunisian coast, but they all managed to find an airfield and land, the first bomber touching down at 1728 GMT, more than eleven hours after take-off. Beirne Lay's *Piccadilly Lily* came in forty-five minutes later:

> At 1815 hours, with red lights showing on all the fuel tanks in my ship, the seven B-17s of the Group which were still in formation circled over a North African airdrome and landed. Our crew was unscratched. Sole damage to the airplane: a bit of ventilation round the tail from flak and 20-mm shells. We slept on the hard ground under the wings of our B-17, but the good earth felt softer than a silk pillow...

Meanwhile, in the early afternoon, as the 4th Wing headed for North Africa after enduring its agony en route to Regensburg, the 230 B-17s of the 1st Wing, organized into four combat wings, were thundering in over the mouth of the Scheldt on their way to Schweinfurt. Leading the mission was the 91st Group, in one of whose Fortresses flew the 1st Wing's Commander, Brigadier General Robert B. Williams.

On this occasion the Luftwaffe fighters, encouraged by their victories that morning, did not wait for the Thunderbolt escort to turn back before launching the first of their attacks. While a strong force of Focke-Wulfs engaged the fighter escort, a second attacked the bombers as they approached the German frontier. Among the first to engage them was No. 5 Squadron of Jagdgeschwader 11, flying Messerschmitt 109s with 21-cm rockets in tubes fitted under their wings. The missiles were not very accurate and most missed their targets by a wide margin, but some struck home and a pair of Fortresses exploded in mid-air, their debris fluttering down.

The B-17s closely followed the route taken by the Regensburg force as far as Mannheim, when they veered sharply northwards to their target. Visibility was still good, and although the bombing was not as accurate as that at Regensburg substantial damage was nevertheless inflicted on the factories, which produced about half Germany's supply of ball-bearings.

The cost, however, was high. Three hundred German fighters harried the B-17s on their way to Schweinfurt and back again, the Focke-Wulfs and Messerschmitts attacking from all quarters. This time, the enemy fighters concentrated on the leading groups, diving out of the sun to rake the topmost group – the 91st – and continuing through the American formation at high speed to hit the bottom group, in this case the 381st. The figures alone testify to the awful efficiency of the German fighter tactics: the 91st Group lost ten B-17s out of twenty-one, and the 381st Group eleven.

These losses accounted for practically one-third of the B-17s destroyed during the Schweinfurt mission: a total of thirty-six bombers. Together with those lost in the Regensburg attack, this meant that sixty Fortresses of VIII Bomber Command had failed to return from the day's operations. Added to this total, a further hundred B-17s had been damaged by flak or fighters, some of them so badly that they had to be scrapped.

In terms of human beings, the day's loss meant that six hundred young men had gone down, a few to survive when they parachuted from their stricken aircraft, others to be picked up from the sea by Allied air-sea rescue craft. The casualty figures did not include those dead and dying airmen who came home in the bullet and splinter-riddled fuselage of their bombers.

Crews returning from both the Regensburg and Schweinfurt missions claimed that they had destroyed 288 enemy fighters – in other words, almost the whole of the Luftwaffe fighter force committed that day. Later, after an Intelligence assessment, the claim was reduced to 148.

The truth was somewhat different. The fierce air battles over Germany and the Low Countries that day had cost the Luftwaffe only twenty-five fighters. It was not hard to understand the vast discrepancy: in the heat of battle, two or three dozen Fortress gunners might take a shot at the same fighter, and if it fell in flames each would claim it as his own.

The high cost of the 'Anniversary Raids' administered a severe jolt to VIII Bomber Command, and it was to be five weeks before the American heavy bombers once again ventured into Germany. General Eaker, however, was determined to pursue his long-range daylight strategic bombing programme with the utmost vigour, and the deep-penetration raids got under way again in October.

The result was a disaster that overshadowed even Regensburg and Schweinfurt. Between 8 and 14 October, when the Americans attacked Bremen, Marienburg, Danzig and Munster and went back to make a second strike on Schweinfurt, they lost 148 bombers and nearly 1,500 aircrew. In the Schweinfurt attack, carried out on 14 October, German fighters and flak destroyed 60 out of the 280 bombers committed – more than twenty per cent of the attacking force.

RAF Spitfire pilots, sent out to escort the returning bombers on the last leg of the flight home, saw harrowing sights:

> It was a clear afternoon, and we first saw their contrails many miles away, as well as the thinner darting contrails of

the enemy fighters above and on either flank. As we closed the gap we could see that they had taken a terrible mauling, for there were gaping holes in their precise formations. Some Fortresses were gradually losing height, and a few stragglers, lagging well behind, were struggling to get home on three engines.

We swept well behind the stragglers and drove off a few 109s and 110s, but the great air battle was over, and what a fight it must have been, because more than half the bombers we nursed over the North Sea were shot up. One or two ditched in the sea, and many others, carrying dead and badly injured crew members, had to make crash-landings. How we longed for more drop tanks, so that some of the many hundreds of Spitfires based in Britain could play their part in the great battles over Germany...

The words of the fighter pilots could easily have applied to the sights they witnessed as the shattered American formations returned from the earlier raid on Schweinfurt.

Here and there in the Fortress formations there were gaps. From close to you could see machines with one, sometimes two stationary engines and feathered propellers. Others had lacerated tailplanes, gaping holes in the fuselages, wings tarnished by fire or glistening with black oil oozing from gutted engines.

Behind the formation were the stragglers, making for the coast, for the haven of refuge of an advanced air base on the other side of the Channel, flying only by a sublime effort of the will. You could imagine the blood pouring over the heaps of empty cartridges, the pilot nursing his remaining engines and anxiously eyeing the long white trail of petrol escaping from his riddled tanks...

Such, in the summer and autumn of 1943, was the martyrdom of the US VIII Bomber Command. Later, in 1944, the daylight bombers would be escorted by long-range P-51 Mustang fighters, and from that time onwards the fortunes of the air war over Europe would start to swing firmly in the Allies' favour. But during those terrible months of

1943 it was courage alone that took the American crews through to their targets week after week: and courage was not enough.

Chapter 11

Ploeşti: the Raid that Failed

At dawn on 1 August 1943, 179 four-engined B-24 Liberator bombers of the United States Army Air Force thundered away from air bases in North Africa and set course over the Mediterranean on the first stage of a 2,000-mile round trip to Romania. Their objective was the big complex of oil refineries at Ploeşti, near Bucharest, which was believed to supply some sixty per cent of the oil requirements of Germany and her European satellites. The bombers were to make their attack at low level, taking the enemy defences by surprise and shattering the target in a carefully-timed strike that was designed to cripple a large part of Germany's war effort in one blow.

The whole plan, however, was destined to go badly awry. Far from being the death blow from which the enemy would never recover, the Ploeşti raid was to turn into one of the biggest disasters ever suffered by the USAAF.

Known as Operation Statesman, the story of the Ploeşti mission began during the last week of June 1943, when three B-24 Groups of VIII Bomber Command – the 44th, 93rd and 389th – left their bases in the United Kingdom and flew to North Africa, where they came under the temporary control of IX Bomber Command. As yet, only a handful of people knew the true nature of the mission, although crews speculated that it might involve low-level work because the advanced Norden bombsights had been removed from their aircraft and replaced by a more rudimentary type which was actually a modified gunsight. Extra bomb-bay fuel tanks had also been hurriedly fitted, together with heavier nose armament.

The Consolidated B-24 Liberator seemed to be the ideal machine to carry out the Ploeşti raid. Powered by four 1,200 hp Pratt and Whitney radial engines, the big twin-finned bomber had a range of well over 2,000 miles, considerably longer than that of the B-17 Flying Fortress, and could carry a normal bomb load of 5,000 lbs. It carried a crew of twelve and a formidable defensive armament of ten

.5-inch machine-guns. In fact, a force of Liberators had already set out to attack Ploeşti once before, in 1942, but that mission had been flown in darkness and poor weather and the bombers had returned to North Africa without locating the target.

It was apparent that, if the Liberators were to pull off a major success, the mission would have to be flown in daylight. No one denied that it would be highly dangerous, but the route to the oil refineries was thought to be lightly defended and the mission's low-level nature should, with luck, give the bombers a sufficient element of surprise to enable them to get through to the target without suffering too heavily.

The attack was not carried out immediately, because on their arrival in North Africa the Liberators were called upon to fly several missions against Italian targets – mainly communications – in support of the Allied invasion of Sicily. The last two weeks of July were spent in training, carrying out mock attacks on targets deep in the desert.

The mission was finally scheduled for Sunday, 1 August 1943, the B-24 groups from England combining with others from IX Bomber Command to make up the required attacking force. The whole mission was to be under the overall control of Major-General Lewis Hyde Brereton, commander of the US Ninth Air Force, and he left the crews in no doubt that their task would be attended by considerable peril. 'We expect our losses to be fifty per cent,' he told them, 'but even though we should lose everything we've sent, but hit the target, it will be well worth it.' The statement was not exactly calculated to raise the morale of the crews; from that moment on, many of them began to resign themselves to the fact that they were not going to come back from Ploeşti.

Take-off on 1 August began at 7:10 a.m. The first group to get airborne was the 376th of IX Bomber Command, led by Colonel Keith K. Compton; next came the 93rd under Colonel Addison Baker; then another unit of the Ninth, the 98th under Colonel John Kane. It was here that the mission suffered its first setback, for one of the 98th's Liberators crashed on take-off from Benina and exploded, killing all those on board. The last two groups to take off were the 44th, led by Colonel Leon Johnson, and Colonel Jack Wood's 389th.

Eleven of the bombers aborted for various technical reasons not long after take-off. The remainder of the five groups involved droned on over the Mediterranean. Then, at 9:50, disaster struck again when the B-24 carrying the navigator of the 376th Group, Captain Anderson, suddenly faltered and spun down into the sea.

It was the first link in a frightening chain of circumstances which, before long, was to enmesh the entire mission. Because the bombers were keeping strict radio silence, there ensued several minutes of confusion following the loss of Anderson's B-24 while the others tried to decide who should now lead. In the end the Liberator flown by Colonel Compton, commander of the 376th, jockeyed its way into the lead position and Compton's navigator assumed responsibility for leading the group to the target. Compton's B-24 also carried, as an observer, General Ent, the chief of IX Bomber Command.

At 12:20 the bombers began crossing Albanian territory, and as they reached Yugoslavia they found heavy cloud cover adding to their navigational problems. Also, the Liberators' carefully planned tight formation, designed to afford the maximum defensive firepower, became badly dislocated as the groups lost sight of each other. Nevertheless, the two leading groups crossed the Romanian border exactly on schedule and set course for their first turning-point: Piteşti, some sixty miles west of their target. The three groups that followed them, however, got into a complete muddle in the cloudy conditions and lost a lot of valuable time as they circled over the Danube, trying to sort themselves into some kind of order. When they finally set course once more, they were twenty minutes late.

Meanwhile, the leading 376th and 93rd Groups went down to two hundred feet and thundered across the Romanian countryside, causing peasants at work in the harvest fields to scatter in panic. As they flashed past Piteşti they came down even lower, drumming over rooftops at a height of less than fifty feet. The crews retained vivid impressions of people hurling themselves face down; others stood their ground and, in a futile gesture, hurled pitchforks at the speeding bombers. One Liberator pilot had to pull up, quite literally, to avoid hitting a horse and cart, while others flew so low – perhaps inad- vertently – that they found corn stalks jammed into crevices on the undersides of their aircraft on their return to base.

From Piteşti, the plan called for the Liberators to fly due east, past Targovişte and then on to Floreşti. From there they were to turn south-east and follow the railway line to Ploeşti. This route would bring them in towards the target area from the north, and each crew had been briefed to pick out its assigned target from this direction. They had spent weeks poring over maps and photographs of Ploeşti, and were confident that they would have little difficulty in locating their objectives.

They had reckoned, however, without the chain of misfortune which was dogging the mission. When the two leading groups reached Targovişte, they sighted a railway leading south, and both Compton and Ent decided that this was the one that would bring them to Ploeşti. Their young navigator, an inexperienced second lieutenant, protested that they had made a grave error and were mistaking Targovişte for Floreşti, but the two senior officers remained adamant and overrode him.

So Compton's Liberator, followed by sixty other bombers, turned to follow the line, unaware that it led not to Ploeşti but to Bucharest. It was only when the tall spires of the Romanian capital emerged through the haze that Compton and Ent realized their mistake, but by then it was too late. The enemy flak batteries were standing by and Focke-Wulfs and Messerschmitts were taking off from just about every airfield in the Balkans. Realizing that it was now utterly pointless to maintain radio silence, General Ent called up the other crews and told them that he was making a left turn towards Ploești. This would bring the bombers up against the southern edge of the refinery complex, an approach angle on which none of the crews had been briefed.

Addison Baker's 93rd Group, in fact, had already realized their mistake and had turned back some minutes earlier; they would be the first over the target area. Meanwhile, the enemy defences were really getting geared up to strike hard at the attacking bombers. At first, the Germans and Romanians had been puzzled when the Liberators were reported to be heading for Bucharest; they could not understand why the Americans should want to attack an innocent city which had no military value whatsoever. Then, when Ent broke radio silence and the two leading bomber groups turned towards Ploești, they knew the answer.

In the meantime, the other three groups had reached Pitești. While the 398th veered off to port to make an individual attack on the refineries at Campina, fifteen miles north-west of Ploești, the others flew on to Florești and turned on to the correct track for the target area.

As they approached from the north, the 93rd and 376th Groups were sweeping in on a converging course from the south, already running the gauntlet of intense flak. With two large formations of bombers speeding towards one another at a closing speed of nearly 600 mph, all flying at about the same height, the stage was set for disaster. As the 93rd and 376th Groups reached the target area, German flak batteries laid a barrage in their path, filling the sky with every conceivable kind of shell. Out of the 93rd Group, no more than five aircraft succeeded in bombing the primary target, such was the utter confusion; the rest dropped their loads more or less at random over a wide area. The Liberator carrying Colonel Addison Baker was shot down over the edge of the target seconds after releasing its bombs and ten more aircraft of the 93rd went down, one of them crashing into a women's prison.

While the 93rd was being shot to pieces, Compton had brought the 376th Group round in a wide twenty-mile semicircle to try and arrive over Ploeşti from the correct angle. The flak, however, rose to meet them with incredible ferocity, and General Ent, realizing at last that the carefully laid attack plan had been torn to shreds, ordered the 376th's crews to attack whatever target they thought fit. This meant that the decision now rested on the shoulders of the group's five squadron commanders, each of whom led six Liberators, and they were not slow to act. The CO of one squadron, Major Appold, selected the Concordia Vega installation and took his six B-24s howling overhead, all releasing their bombs at the same time. The effect was spectacular, the oil storage tanks exploding in boiling flame and smoke. The six Liberators emerged from the spreading black pall covered in soot, but otherwise miraculously unharmed. This, in fact, was the target that had been reserved for Addison Baker's 93rd Group.

Meanwhile, the 44th Group under Colonel Leon Johnson and the 98th led by Colonel John Kane were crossing the outer fringes of the target area at the end of their approach from the north.

The group commanders had no idea that a serious blunder had been made until they saw several Liberators of the 376th Group flash beneath them from the wrong direction, heading south-west, and observed that several of the targets earmarked for attack by the 44th and 98th had already been bombed. This meant that both groups had to fly directly into a holocaust of smoke and flame, running the risk of being destroyed in the explosions of delayed-action bombs. But there was no alternative: the Liberators bored in, the pilots steering blindly through sheets of flame that rose to heights of five hundred feet and more. The great bombers were tossed about the sky like corks in the fearful turbulence; some pilots lost control and dived into the ground, others were incinerated in vast explosions. 'We all felt sick when we saw the oil tanks exploding,' commented one of the pilots who survived. 'Somebody ahead had bombed our target by mistake. There was nothing to do but try and hit it again; there was no time for another run on this trip.'

One pilot of the 98th, Captain John Palm, saw the other five Liberators of his squadron go down in flames one after the other. He was the only one to reach the target, and as he approached it three of his engines were hit and knocked out. A second later a flak shell burst in the bomber's nose, killing two crew members outright and severing Palm's right leg. With his bomber losing height fast he managed to pull the emergency bomb release just in time. Then he slammed the Liberator down in a corn-field and dragged himself painfully out of the wreck through a cockpit window. Palm and several other crew members survived and were taken prisoner by the Romanians, who treated them well.

In theory, the easiest objective assigned to any Group that day was the Steaua Română refinery at Campina, the target of Jack Wood's 389th. Ground fire, however, proved exceptionally heavy, and a running battle developed between the Liberators' gunners and enemy machine-gun nests emplaced on the sides of hills. The bombers had to pass through a valley to reach their objective, and for a time they were so low that the enemy guns were actually firing down on them. One bomber, flown by Second Lieutenant Lloyd Hughes, was hit repeatedly and staggered on with white petrol vapour streaming from its ruptured tanks. As Hughes passed over the target and released his bombs, his aircraft passed through a sheet of flame which ignited the escaping fuel. With the whole of the port wing ablaze, Hughes tried desperately to make a forced landing, but the B-24 stalled and crashed. The whole sequence was captured by an official cameraman travelling on another B-24 – one of the most remarkable films to be shot during the Second World War.

A few minutes later Campina was also hit by some Liberators of the 376th Group, searching for targets of opportunity.

The Liberators turned away on the first leg of the long flight back, the sky behind them dark with mushrooming smoke. It was now that the enemy fighters pounced on them: Focke-Wulfs and Messerschmitts of I/JG 4 under Captain Hans Hahn, IV/JG 27 led by First Lieutenant Burk, and Captain Lutje's IV/NJG 6. The latter was a night-fighter unit, flying twin-engined Messerschmitt 110s. The Romanian Air Arm was engaged, too, flying a mixture of modern IAR-80 radial-engined fighters and a miscellany of older aircraft, including a few Gloster Gladiator biplanes supplied to Romania by Britain in 1935. The latter proved more dangerous than expected, flying over the

Liberators at top speed and dropping showers of fragmentation bombs on them. Several bombers were reported to have been lost when these small but deadly missiles shattered their wings or tail units. As the Liberators flew south, Italian fighter squadrons also harried them.

At first the bombers were comparatively safe from serious attack. As long as they stayed at low level the enemy fighters found it difficult to engage them, but as soon as they climbed to cross the mountains the slaughter began. One by one the B-24s went down in flames, and as soon as one enemy fighter squadron broke off the action it was replaced by another. Precious fuel was used up as the American pilots manoeuvred desperately to avoid the determined fighter attacks, with the result that few of the survivors managed to regain their North African bases. Some limped into Cyprus and Sicily; others made emergency landings in neutral Turkey, where their crews were interned.

The Ploeşti Raid brought the award of five Congressional Medals of Honor. One of them, posthumously, went to Lieutenant-Colonel Addison Baker, commander of the 93rd. After a shell struck the cockpit of Baker's bomber on the run-in to the target, injuring himself and his co-pilot, Baker had stuck rigidly to his course, even though a second heavy shell turned the Liberator into a mass of flame. He held control just long enough to get his bombs away, then apparently – according to eye-witness reports – tried to pull the stricken bomber up steeply so that the crew could attempt to bale out. Instead the Liberator had turned a few fast somersaults, like a giant blazing Catherine wheel, and dived into the ground with the loss of all on board. The eye-witness told how that last steep climb, with the Liberator in such a crippled condition, must have needed all the strength of two men pulling back on the control columns, so the inference was that Baker's co-pilot, Major John Jerstad, must have been helping. Jerstad was also awarded a posthumous Medal of Honor. So was the gallant young Lloyd Hughes of the 389th, who had made such a fierce attempt to save his crew after bombing Campina.

The fourth Medal of Honor recipient was Colonel Leon Johnson of the 44th, who, on finding that his assigned target had already been attacked, had stayed in the target area for some considerable time in search of another before finally setting course for home. Despite the severe damage inflicted on his Liberator, the *Suzy-Q*, Johnson brought her safely through to the Mediterranean with one other aircraft of the 44th Group, Captain W. R. Cameron's *Buzzin' Bear*. These two Liberators were the only ones of the group's 66th and 67th Bomb Squadrons – seventeen aircraft in all – which managed to regain their base at Benina. The others had either been shot down or had made emergency landings elsewhere.

For most crews, that long flight back across the Mediterranean was a nightmare. After being attacked by a strong formation of enemy fighters, the Liberator flown by Colonel Kane of the 98th Group had the housing around the propeller and three cylinders of its No. 4 engine shot to pieces and the propeller on the No. 1 engine shattered, the flying fragments slicing a hole in the aileron. To make matters worse, fuel was leaking from one of the wing tanks. The bomber staggered away from the target area on three engines, one of which was running roughly, and about two hundred miles south of the refineries the crew suddenly realized that they had no hope of making it back to North Africa. The navigator, Lieutenant Norman

Whalen, therefore worked out a course for the nearest Allied airfield, which was on Cyprus.

Accompanied by two other damaged Liberators, Kane's bomber staggered south at a few miles an hour above stalling speed. At one point it had to climb to get above a mountain range, so the crew threw out every movable object – oxygen bottles and masks, ammunition, radio and anything else they could dismantle – in an effort to reduce weight. They scraped through the mountains at 7,000 feet, avoiding the higher peaks by flying through valleys. They landed in Cyprus at 9:10 p.m., exactly fourteen hours and forty minutes after they had left Africa that morning.

Others were not so lucky. One Liberator, flown by Lieutenant Gilbert Hadley and named *Hadley's Harem*, also tried to reach Cyprus with two engines out of action and two members of the crew killed by flak bursts. They got through the mountains safely, and were at 5,000 feet over the Aegean Sea when a third engine gave up the ghost. There was no alternative but to ditch, and as Hadley brought her down water poured into her through dozens of splinter-holes in her fuselage, dragging her quickly under the surface. Hadley and his co-pilot were trapped in the cockpit and drowned; the seven survivors dragged themselves out of the wreckage with great difficulty and managed to reach the Turkish shore, which was less than a mile away.

As soon as they waded on to the beach they found themselves surrounded by Turkish peasants, armed to the teeth with ancient rifles, who built a huge fire and mounted guard all night while the airmen slept. The next morning, the Americans were resigned to the fact that they would shortly be interned when they were suddenly sighted by a low-flying RAF Wellington patrol aircraft. Within a short time an air-sea rescue launch arrived from Cyprus and the Americans were taken on board.

Crews who did manage to reach an Allied airfield, in North Africa or elsewhere, seemed numb with shock. White-faced and trembling with fatigue after their long ordeal, they told horrifying stories of Liberators crashing in flames over Ploeşti, of great bombers smashed like matchwood into burning fragments, of blazing wreckage scattered across the countryside between the target area and the sea, of bombers exploding in mid-air over the refineries as they flew through soaring whirlpools of fire.

It was time to count the cost. Of the 179 Liberators dispatched on the raid, eleven had aborted and two had crashed, leaving 166 to attack the target. Of these, 53 had failed to return and most of the others were damaged. In human terms, 440 men were killed or missing, many others were wounded and about two hundred were prisoners of war.

It was too high a price to pay, and the crews who did get back – together with a lot of Americans in high places – were understandably eager to pin the blame on those who had planned the raid. The facts, however, were different. The attack plan had been good; the trouble was that it had relied too much on accurate timing, which was very difficult to achieve over such a distance even in the most favourable of conditions. It had also failed to take into account the extent of the enemy opposition. Even then, most of the casualties had been caused not by fighters, but by intense ground fire, and with targets the size of Liberators flying only a few feet off the ground the enemy gunners had found it almost impossible to miss.

The planners were not to blame; even though the attack had perhaps been over-ambitious and had placed too much confidence on the skill of the crews, it had certainly not been suicidal. The crews themselves had not been to blame either; they were inexperienced in low-flying techniques, they suffered from a number of common USAAF procedures such as that of having a single lead navigator in charge of a formation without adequate backup in case he was lost, and the result was apparent when the groups became split up in cloud. Also, in one or two cases, crews had suffered from having too many chiefs and not enough Indians, as when Compton and Ent had overruled their navigator.

However, there was no escaping the fact that whatever the contributory factors had been, the raid had been a total disaster, albeit one through which acts of individual heroism shone like stars. The oil refineries, though badly hit, were soon in operation again and their output quickly reached its former level.

The disaster brought an effective halt to deep-penetration daylight missions over southern Europe by the USAAF until long-range escort fighters became available in 1944. There were to be more heavy raids on Ploeşti that year, but on those occasions the bombers were operating from bases in Italy and escorted by long-range Mustang fighters. Yet the oil refineries were never brought to a stand-still; they were still producing oil when the Russian armies rolled over them in August 1944.

Chapter 12

Nürnberg: the Night-Fighters' Triumph

No. 578 Squadron was destined to be one of the shortest-lived units in the history of the Royal Air Force. It was formed at Snaith, in Yorkshire, on 14 January 1944 as a heavy bomber unit and equipped with Halifax IIIs; it would be disbanded just fifteen months later, on 15 April 1945, before the war in Europe ended.

In that short time, however, the squadron had a distinguished career. Its aircraft flew over 2,700 sorties, dropped 9,676 tons of bombs on the enemy and expended 9,550 rounds of ammunition in air combat. Two of its Halifaxes logged over a hundred missions each, a comparative rarity, and one of its pilots was awarded the Victoria Cross.

The night was 30–31 March 1944, the pilot's name was Pilot Officer Cyril Barton, and the target was Nürnberg. The following day, the name of that distant Bavarian town would be repeated with shock and disbelief throughout Britain as people tuned in to the BBC news bulletins and heard a grim-voiced announcer tell the world that ninety-five heavy bombers had failed to return from the most disastrous raid ever undertaken by Bomber Command.

The flight to the target across darkened Europe had been a nightmare. All the way from the Dutch coast, Barton's crew had seen burning bombers falling from the sky like comets. When they were seventy miles from Nürnberg, they were themselves attacked by a Junkers 88 night-fighter, whose first burst of fire wrecked the bomber's intercom system and put both the rear and mid-upper turrets out of action. A few minutes later a second fighter, a Messerschmitt 210, also joined the battle and its cannon shells damaged one of the bomber's engines.

Fighters continued to make sporadic attacks on the Halifax as it approached the target, causing further damage, and with their guns out of action there was no way in which the crew could retaliate. A great deal of understandable confusion occurred as they tried to communicate with shouts and hand signals; in the middle of it the navigator, bombardier and wireless operator misinterpreted one of Barton's gestures and all three baled out before anyone could stop them.

Barton now had to face a situation of extreme danger. His aircraft was damaged, three vital members of his crew had gone and he was unable to communicate with those who remained. If he continued the mission, he would be at the mercy of hostile fighters when his bomber was silhouetted against the fires in the target area, and if he survived he would have to make a four-and-a-half hour journey home on three engines, doing all the navigating himself.

Cyril Barton would have been quite justified in jettisoning his bomb load and turning for home there and then. Instead he decided to press home his attack at all costs and flew on to Nürnberg, using the emergency release to drop his bombs on the burning city.

As Barton turned for home, the propeller of the damaged engine, which had been vibrating badly, suddenly flew off. Shortly afterwards, the flight engineer discovered that two of the Halifax's fuel tanks were holed and leaking, diminishing the bomber's chances of reaching home.

Somehow, Barton managed to hold his course, even though he was completely lacking in navigational aids and the bomber now had to battle through a strong headwind. Avoiding the most dangerous defence areas on his route, he eventually crossed the English coast some ninety miles north of 578 Squadron's base. By this time the fuel was almost exhausted, and before the exhausted pilot could find a suitable airfield the port engine stopped.

The Halifax was now at a very low altitude, and with only two engines still functioning there could be no question of climbing so that the rest of the crew could bale out. Barton therefore ordered them to take up their crash stations, and seconds later another engine failed. Using the power of the sole remaining engine, the pilot made a gallant attempt to clear some houses and the bomber crash-landed in the fields beyond. Barton lost his life, but the three remaining crew members survived to tell of his heroism.

The tragedy of the Nürnberg raid was, in a way, the result of the big RAF attack on Hamburg the previous July. After Hamburg, German night-fighter tactics were completely revised and new night-fighter units were formed to employ new techniques against the night raiders. One such unit was Jagdgeschwader 300, commanded by Major Hajo Hermann. Equipped with single-engined Focke-Wulf 190s and Messerschmitt 109s, its task was to patrol directly over the German cities, the fighter pilots attacking any bomber they managed to pick out against the glare of the fires below.

These tactics – known as 'Wilde Sau' (Wild Boar) – cost Bomber Command 123 aircraft destroyed and 114 damaged during three major raids on Berlin in August and September 1943, giving the Luftwaffe's night-fighter arm its first real victory of the war. However, these 'Wilde Sau' successes were achieved on clear summer nights, when the German fighter pilots, cruising at high altitude, had little difficulty in locating their targets. During the winter months, with their attendant bad weather, the fighters' success rate dropped sharply, and accidents on landing or take-off took a severe toll. On one occasion, twenty-five out of sixty fighters dispatched on operations were destroyed in a single night, most of them accidentally.

Nevertheless, Hermann's 'Wilde Sau' units, which finally reverted to the day-fighter role in

April 1944, filled a big gap in the Luftwaffe's night defences while work on more advanced radio and radar equipment continued under conditions of high priority during the autumn of 1943. In October that year, German night-fighter units began to re-equip with a new airborne interception radar, the FUG 220 Lichtenstein SN-2, which was free from both electronic and Window interference. Its maximum range was four miles, and it was not long before some night-fighter crews began to score a formidable number of successes with its aid.

More serious still for Bomber Command, by the end of 1943 the Germans were using two new homing devices, the FUG 350 Naxos Z and the FUG 227 Flensburg. The former enabled the Luftwaffe night-fighters to home on to H2S transmissions, and the latter could lock on to radiations from the new 'Monica' tail warning radar which was now fitted to the RAF's heavy bombers. This meant that in the winter of 1943–44, RAF bomber crews using H2S and Monica were actually advertising their presence to the enemy, with disastrous consequences.

It was not until well into 1944 that the Allies assembled sufficient information on these new devices to bring effective countermeasures into play, and in the meantime the enemy night-fighters enjoyed a success they had never achieved so far in the war, and would never achieve again. Moreover, they achieved it with two types of aircraft which had been in service since the start of the war, the Junkers 88 and the Messerschmitt Bf 110.

Both these types formed the backbone of the Luftwaffe's night-fighter force at the end of 1943, although the C.-in-C., General Joseph Kammhuber, had been pressing for the production of a specialized night-fighter throughout that year. This was the Heinkel He 219 Uhu (Owl), which had flown in November 1942 but which had subsequently languished through lack of interest on the part of the German Air Ministry. Interest, however, rapidly reawakened after the Hamburg attacks, and the aircraft was ordered into production. Kammhuber wanted 2,000, but in the event only a tenth of that number was built before the end of the war. The He 219 was a potent machine, equipped with all the latest radar interception aids and six 20-mm cannon, and had it been available in quantity it would undoubtedly have wrought havoc among the RAF's night-bomber force during 1944.

As it was, the Luftwaffe was forced to rely on the conversion of existing designs to the night-fighter role. Despite all the problems this entailed, several innovations had been brought into use by the end of 1943 which made the German night-fighters formidable adversaries. One of them was an ingenious gun mounting known as 'Schrage Musik', which literally meant slanting music. Devised by a sergeant armourer named Paul Mahle (who, incidentally, had served on Messerschmitt 110 units since the beginning of the war) it involved the mounting of two 20-mm cannon, their muzzles pointing upward at a fixed angle, on a wooden platform in the upper fuselage of a night-fighter. This arrangement enabled the fighter to take advantage of a bomber's blind spot and to attack it from directly below with the aid of a reflector sight mounted in the cockpit roof.

The Luftwaffe unit that pioneered the use of Schrage Musik was II/NJG 5, operating Messerschmitt 110s, and the device was first used operationally on the night of 17–18 August during a big RAF attack on the German rocket research centre at Peenemünde on the Baltic coast. On that occasion, the night-fighters destroyed six British bombers in the space of thirty minutes, and they shot down eighteen more during the next eight weeks.

Although hamstrung to a great extent by problems of reequipment and reorganisation, the Luftwaffe night-fighter force attained its biggest successes in the early weeks of 1944. In the course of three big air battles over Germany, Bomber Command suffered crippling losses. On the night of 19–20 February, 78 out of a force of 823 heavy bombers dispatched to attack Leipzig failed to return, while 72 more were destroyed during a big assault on Berlin on 24–25 March.

At this stage in the war, with an Allied invasion of western Europe only weeks away and the Germans suffering serious reverses on every battlefront, the German people were badly in need of a victory, and a victory against the Allied strategic bomber force would be the best kind of all. By day, the Allies had established a firm degree of air superiority, with long-range Mustang fighters escorting the massive phalanxes of Flying Fortresses and Liberators to targets deep inside Germany and inflicting substantial losses on the Luftwaffe's day-fighter force; a victory here would be hard to achieve unless it was with the aid of the new Messerschmitt 262 jet fighters, and the production of these had been subjected to such endless delays that they would not be available in any significant numbers for a long time.

If there was to be a major Luftwaffe victory, therefore, it would have to be scored by the night-fighter force. Such an achievement was well within its potential, even with the equipment in service at the beginning of 1944. All that was needed was a set of favourable circumstances, and in March 1944, due to a combination of bad luck and unimaginative planning that was quite uncharacteristic at this time, Bomber Command was about to present the German night-fighters with an extraordinary opportunity.

In the evening of 30 March 795 Lancasters and Halifaxes took off from their bases in Yorkshire and East Anglia and set course south-eastwards across the North Sea. Their target was the vital industrial centre and railway junction of Nürnberg, deep in the heart of southern Germany.

There was no detour; the bombers headed straight for the enemy coast near Bruges, crossing Belgium to a point slightly to the north of

Charleroi. Later, for some reason which is still unclear to this day, the official Bomber Command report stated that no diversionary raids were carried out that night because of 'conditions in the North Sea'. This was simply not true; conditions were calm and clear, the night was moonlit and diversionary attacks were carried out by small forces of Mosquitoes on several enemy airfields in Holland.

Reports of these attacks began to reach the headquarters of the Luftwaffe's 1st Air Division at 10 p.m., but the General Officer Commanding I Fighter Corps, Major-General Josef Schmid, recognized them for what they were and decided to keep his night-fighter force on the ground with the pilots at five minutes' readiness. Then, at 10:30, the German coastal radar stations detected a major raid building up over the Norfolk coast, and a few minutes later the head of the bomber stream was reported to be heading south-eastwards towards Belgium.

Schmid finally 'scrambled' the first of his night-fighters at 11 p.m., once the track of the bomber stream had been firmly established over Belgium. They caught up with the bombers at the latter's turning-point north of Charleroi and shot two of them down within five minutes. Much worse, however, was still to come.

From Charleroi, the bomber stream turned on to a new track, a 250-mile long straight line bearing due east to Fulda, northeast of Frankfurt. This track ran close to two radio beacons, one code-named 'Ida' to the south of Aachen and the other, beacon 'Otto', east of Frankfurt, both of which were used as assembly-points by German night-fighter units. At this stage, the Germans had no idea where the bombers were heading. They only knew that Bomber Command had developed the technique of diversion and course-change to a fine art, and that the present raid might suddenly switch to a new heading without warning. (Long after the war, it was alleged that the Germans already knew the target, either through a security leak or an inadvertent radio transmission from one of the aircraft involved. It was even suggested that details of the target had been deliberately leaked by British Intelligence to lend credibility to an agent who had the task of planting false information about the coming Allied invasion of Europe. There is, however, no real evidence to support any of these allegations.)

Major-General Schmid had no intention of splitting up his night-fighter forces piecemeal. Instead, he reasoned that whichever way the bomber stream turned, it would have to pass close to one or other of the two radio beacons. He therefore ordered his night-fighters to concentrate there, the squadrons of 3 Fighter Division taking station over beacon 'Ida' and those of Colonel Hajo Hermann's 1 Fighter Division flying south to beacon 'Otto', together with the fighters of Major-General Max Ibel's 2 Fighter Division.

So, largely because of a combination of astute reasoning and sheer luck, the stage was set for a major catastrophe. Other factors were to contribute to it, too, among them the weather conditions. The night was very clear, with a half moon, and the freezing level was lower than usual. This meant that many of the bombers, flying at altitudes of between 16,000 and 22,000 feet, were leaving long condensation trails in their wake, shining brightly in the moonlight. This was one night when the night-fighters had no trouble in locating their targets.

As the bombers' track passed Aachen and beacon 'Ida', the fighters of Major-General Walter Grabmann's 3 Fighter Division got into the bomber stream and the slaughter began. Armed with their 'Schrage Musik', the Messerschmitt 110s and Junkers 88s, guided to their targets either by their radar operators or the clearly-visible contrails streaming behind the bombers' engines, crept up beneath the Lancasters and Halifaxes and opened fire.

This was the heavy bombers' blind spot; there was no ventral gun position, and the rear-gunner's downward field of vision was restricted. All the night-fighter pilot had to do was manoeuvre until the bomber's great black shadow filled his sights overhead, and press the firing-button. Usually, the German pilots tried to aim for the bombers' wings, with their vulnerable fuel tanks; a number of night-fighters had been lost when their shells ripped into the bomb-bay of their victim, obliterating both aircraft in one shattering explosion.

By the time the bombers reached Siegen, sixty miles northwest of Frankfurt, twenty-four of them had already been shot flaming from the sky, and still the nightmare went on. As 3 Fighter Division's crews broke off the action and returned to their bases to refuel and rearm, their place was taken by units of 1 and 2 Fighter Divisions, which up to now had been orbiting patiently over beacon 'Otto'. The bombers stuck doggedly to their easterly heading, and the fighters smacked down nineteen more of them between Siegen and Münnerstadt, where the whole force suddenly turned south towards its objective.

German night-fighter pilots, some of whom had yet to score their first victory before tonight, suddenly found themselves shooting down one bomber after another. One pilot, First Lieutenant Martin Becker, destroyed no fewer than seven, all of them with 'Schrage Musik'. Flying a Messerschmitt 110 of No. 1 Squadron, Nacht-Jagdgeschwader 6 (I/NJG 6), he took off from his base at Mainz-Finthen at 11:45 p.m., and half an hour later his radar operator brought him into contact with a group of Halifaxes east of Bonn. He destroyed the first of them twenty minutes after midnight and five more in the next half hour. It was not difficult to trace the bombers' route, which was marked by a trail of burning wreckage on the ground far below. Becker returned to base to refuel and rearm, took off again and claimed his seventh victim over Luxembourg at 3:15 a.m.

Two more fighter pilots destroyed four bombers each. They were First Lieutenant Helmut Schulte of II/NJG 5 and Lieutenant Dr Wilhelm Seuss of IV/NJG 5. Another pilot, First Lieutenant Martin Drewes, accounted for three. Between them, therefore, these four men and their crews were responsible for twenty per cent of the total loss sustained by Bomber Command that night.

The merciless harrying of the bomber stream continued as the Halifaxes and Lancasters began their final run towards the target, twelve more being shot down before they reached the city. That brought the total RAF loss so far to fifty-five bombers, and the first bombs had not yet fallen on Nürnberg. It was only now, when the bomber stream entered the last leg of its outward journey, that the Germans knew for certain that Nürnberg was the target. Hajo Hermann's single-engined 'Wilde Sau' fighters were hurriedly ordered into the air, but most of their bases were a considerable distance from Nürnberg and not one of them made contact with the attackers. It was their failure at Nürnberg, in fact, which led to their reversion to pure day-fighting operations a week or so later.

Nevertheless, the twin-engined night-fighters found plenty of targets as the great bombers crawled across the burning city, and combats flared up all over the sky. In the hour or so between the first and last sticks of bombs going down, a further twenty-three bombers had crashed flaming in the immediate area of the target.

As they left Nürnberg the bombers swung south-west towards Stuttgart, then turned west-north-west on a track that took them across the Rhine near Strasbourg on the start of another long, straight leg of about 260 miles to a point south of Reims, where a further slight course correction brought them over the Channel coast near Dieppe. The homeward route lay well to the south of the main concentrations of enemy fighters, but fifteen more aircraft were lost before they reached the sea.

Even then, the bombers' ordeal was not over. The Luftwaffe had sent out a small force of night intruders to patrol the Channel and the bomber bases of East Anglia, and several returning crews reported brief combats. Most of these were indecisive, but one Halifax was shot down in mid-Channel and another on the approach to land at its Norfolk airfield.

The following morning, Bomber Command counted the cost. Ninety-five heavy bombers, with 665 aircrew, had failed to return. Added to that, twelve more bombers had crashed while attempting to land in England; Pilot Officer Cyril Barton's was among them. Another fact which also had to be taken into account was that a further seventy-one bombers had been damaged, many of them seriously, and quite a number had returned to base with dead and seriously wounded crew members on board.

To make the tragedy even harder to bear, only a small proportion of the bombers attacking Nürnberg had managed to place their bombs anywhere near the target area. Attacked repeatedly by fighters, scared stiff by the sight of huge bombers falling like swatted flies all around them, crews had released their bombs more or less at random or had suddenly found themselves forced to take violent evasive action at a crucial point in their bombing runs.

The effect of the Nürnberg disaster on the morale of Bomber Command, already reeling under the succession of heavy losses it had sustained that winter, was ferocious. This new blow, coming as it did at a time when the Allies appeared to be getting the upper hand of the German fighters, had sufficient impact to call a halt to further deep-penetration night attacks by Bomber Command for months to come. Admittedly, beginning in April 1944 and continuing throughout the summer, the major part of the Command's effort was to be devoted to direct support of the Allied landings in Normandy and the subsequent exploitation inland, and it was not until October that large-scale night attacks on German targets were resumed.

Nürnberg, then, brought about a radical change in the RAF's strategic bombing policy. Sir Arthur Harris's scheme for continuing large-scale area attacks on Germany's cities, which had seemed to work so effectively the previous summer, was now shown to be too costly to support when such attacks involved long-range missions by large numbers of bombers. Doubtless, had such attacks persisted, the German night-fighters would have scored other major victories, perhaps matching or even surpassing that of Nürnberg. As it was, Nürnberg was at the same time their greatest achievement, and their swan song.

The biggest major operation carried out by Bomber Command against a German target after

Nürnberg, in fact, took place on 27 August, when 216 bombers attacked an oil plant at Homberg in the Ruhr.

It was a daylight attack; the wheel had turned full circle since 1942. This time, however, there was a difference. The bombers were escorted by a massive formation of Spitfires. It was the first time that Bomber Command had ever crossed the Rhine with fighter cover. From now on, the Lancasters and Halifaxes would no longer have to rely entirely on the cloak of darkness.

Chapter 13

The Earthquake Raids

It was 25th April 1945, and the Thousand-Year Reich was entering its last fourteen days. Russian troops were fighting in the streets of Berlin, while in the west British, American and French armies were rolling from the Rhine past the stark desolation of cities that had been subjected to two years of savage air bombardment by day and night.

In the south, the United States Seventh Army was thrusting deep into Bavaria. The Americans had fought hard, often over difficult terrain, since their landing in southern France in August 1944, and now they were almost within sight of their goal: Hitler's mountain retreat at Berchtesgaden. It was here, over the past decade, that the Führer and his entourage had formulated so many of the plans which had plunged Europe into ruin, and it was here that the Nazis had planned to set up a 'national

253

redoubt' in which they were to make a desperate last-ditch stand. The rapid advance of the Seventh Army had destroyed all hope of bringing such a plan to fruition, but Berchtesgaden was known to be defended by a considerable number of fanatical SS troops, and it was certain that if the place had to be stormed the Americans would suffer many casualties.

On the morning of 25 April eleven Avro Lancaster bombers of No. 617 Squadron, Royal Air Force, took off from their Lincolnshire base of Woodhall Spa and set out on the long flight to Bavaria. Four of the aircraft carried massive 12,000-lb 'Tallboy' bombs, the remainder mixed loads of incendiaries and thousand-pounders. Navigation was difficult, for western Europe was covered by a mantle of snow, and over Bavaria the crews found it almost impossible to identify landmarks. Eight of them located the Obersalzberg mountain, on which Hitler's 'Eagle's Nest' stood, but Berchtesgaden merged with the white hills and low cloud and the bomb-aimers were unable to pinpoint it. However, they managed to identify the SS barracks, and despite the difficult weather conditions these were successfully obliterated by the Tallboys and thousand-pounders. When American troops finally reached Berchtesgaden a week later, they reported that the wooded hillsides were still smouldering from the effects of the attack.

The Berchtesgaden raid was 617 Squadron's last operational mission of World War II. It was a little under two years since it had carried out its first, the famous attack on the Moehne and Eder Dams, and since then it had established a considerable reputation as a precision-attack unit. During the early part of 1944, the squadron had carried out a series of brilliant 'pinpoint' attacks on factories in France, the object being to ensure maximum damage while sparing the lives of French workers. These attacks were led by Wing Commander G. L. Cheshire, who had taken over the squadron at the end of 1943, and whose cold and calculated acceptance of danger was exemplified by his leadership in an attack on Munich in April 1944. This was an experimental attack designed to try out a new method of low-level target marking against a heavily-defended target deep in Germany, and Munich was selected at Cheshire's request simply because of the formidable nature of its anti-aircraft defences. The weather was poor, and to get round the worst of it Cheshire had to fly a route that took him over the defences of Augsburg. From that moment he was almost continuously under fire, and as he reached the target flares dropped by higher-flying Lancasters suddenly burst into brilliant light, illuminating him from above. Searchlights fastened on to him and every gun in the vicinity opened up on him. The fierce light was so blinding that he almost lost control, but he managed to recover in time and dived to seven hundred feet, releasing his markers with great accuracy.

Although his bomber was riddled with shell fragments, Cheshire flew over the target at 1,000 feet for several minutes to ensure that his markers had been accurately placed. Only then did he turn for home, flying through intense fire for a full twelve minutes as he left the target.

Cheshire was later awarded the Victoria Cross. It was an award that was made for sustained effort in the face of great peril over a period of time, rather than for one action, and as such it was unique in the annals of Britain's armed forces. Guy Gibson, 617 Squadron's first VC, had led the unit to fame in the heroic dams raid; Leonard Cheshire was to lead it to new heights of precision in the critical months of 1944.

Precision was certainly the keyword on one of 617's more unusual missions, carried out in the early hours of 6 June 1944 as D-day dawned and an invasion fleet of over 3,000 vessels headed for their objectives on the coast of Normandy. Eight of the squadron's Lancasters flew a series of eight-mile legs over the Channel, each aircraft dropping twelve bundles of 'Window' per minute from a height of 3,000 feet. Code-named Operation Taxable, this mission was a ruse designed to make the enemy think that the invasion forces were about to land north of Le Havre, the 'Window' bundles producing echoes similar to those of a large number of surface vessels on the German radar screens.

Three nights later, 617 Squadron went into action with a formidable new weapon. Known as Tallboy, it was a 12,000-lb bomb designed by Barnes Wallis, architect of the mines which the squadron had used to breach the Moehne and Eder Dams. It was a remarkable weapon, having both the explosive power of a high-capacity blast bomb and the penetrating power of an armour-piercing bomb without sacrificing explosive filling for thickness of casing. Its secret lay in its perfect streamlining, which gave it a terminal velocity of 3,600 feet per second – faster than the speed of sound.

Its use required a high degree of accuracy, because in order to achieve maximum penetration it had to be dropped from a height of 8,000 feet or more. No. 617 Squadron's Lancasters were therefore fitted with new Mk IIA bomb sights, which enabled their highly trained crews to place the bombs within eighty yards of the target from a height of 20,000 feet. This margin of error was quite acceptable, for the exploding Tallboy displaced a million cubic feet of earth and formed a crater that took 5,000 tons of soil to fill. The Lancasters' bomb-bays were also modified to accommodate the lengthy bombs.

Armed with Tallboys, nineteen Lancasters of 617 Squadron set out on the night of 8–9 June 1944 to destroy the Saumur railway tunnel in southern France, a vital point on the main rail artery through which the Germans were bringing reinforcements from the south-west to the Normandy front. Ahead of 617, four Lancasters of No. 83 Squadron were to drop flares over the target so that Wing Commander Cheshire could mark the south-west entrance to the tunnel with red spot fires, after which they were to bomb the railway bridge at the tunnel's other entrance with ordinary thousand-pounders.

Although some of 83 Squadron's flares went wide because of poor H2S indications, they provided sufficient light for Cheshire to sweep in and place his red spot markers within forty yards of the tunnel entrance. The bombardiers in 617's Lancasters, flying at 10,000 feet just under the cloud base, located them without difficulty and released their Tallboys, expecting to see spectacular results. They were disappointed: all they saw was a series of red pinpricks as the six-ton bombs bored into the ground around the markers, and it was not until reconnaissance aircraft returned with photographs the following day that they realized the awesome devastation they had caused.

Seventeen Tallboys had fallen round the tunnel mouth, penetrating deep into the ground and causing enormous craters. An eighteenth had fallen on the railway bridge at the other end of the tunnel. It was the nineteenth bomb, however, that had caused the greatest damage, ripping through the hillside that towered over the tunnel mouth and exploding in the tunnel itself, bringing down something like ten thousand tons of earth.

The tunnel was still blocked two months later, when the area was occupied by American forces.

During the weeks that followed, No. 617 Squadron's Tallboy-equipped Lancasters wrought more destruction on more 'hard' targets, notably the U-boat pens at Brest, Lorient, St Nazaire and La Pallice and the E-boat bases at Le Havre and Boulogne, all of which were protected by thick concrete. Then they struck at the V-1 flying bomb construction sites at Siracourt, Watten, Wizernes and Mimoyecques. The latter attacks were carried out in daylight, with Cheshire marking the object-ives in a newly-acquired P-51 Mustang fighter, and despite heavy flak succeeded in wrecking most of them.

On the night of 23 September 1944 the squadron returned to Germany, when eleven Lancasters led by Wing Commander J. B. Tait — who had taken over as commanding officer from Leonard Cheshire — took off from Woodhall Spa to attack the Dortmund-Ems Canal aqueduct near Munster. Their task was to breach the banks of the canal, whose water level was higher than the level of the surrounding countryside, and drain it. The canal, which carried a large amount of industrial traffic, had been the object of Bomber Command's attentions on several previous occasions, but had always survived more or less intact. Now 617 Squadron was going to try and knock it out once and for all, and just to make sure 125 Lancasters carrying ordinary bomb-loads were to attack it as well.

The target was marked by five Mosquitoes, and despite unfavourable weather conditions, with seven-tenths clouds at between eight and nine thousand feet, the attack was a complete success. The canal was breached and a $6\frac{1}{2}$-mile stretch was completely drained. After that, Bomber Command breached the canal just as often as the Germans repaired it.

No. 617 was really warming up to its 'Tallboy' operations now, and on 7 October it used the bombs in yet another dams raid – although one in no way as spectacular as the famous mission of May 1943. This time the target was the Kembs Dam, which lay on the upper Rhine north of Basle. The Germans had intended to release the enormous volume of water contained by the dam to block the Allied advance across the upper Rhine, but 617 Squadron did the job for them. Seventeen Lancasters, once again led by Wing Commander

Tait, braved a massive anti-aircraft barrage to lay their Tallboys on the dam, shattering its wall and releasing the pent-up waters. By the time the Allied ground forces eventually reached the scene, the floods had subsided. The success, however, was bought at the cost of two Lancasters, one of which exploded over the target with its Tallboy still on board.

During the second week of November No. 617 Squadron carried out a mission which, in its own way, was to attract as much publicity as the famous attack on the Moehne and Eder Dams. The target was the German battleship *Tirpitz*, anchored in Norway's Tromsø Fjord.

The heavily-armed, 45,000-ton *Tirpitz* had presented a serious threat to the Allied North Atlantic convoys for two years, although damage inflicted on her in air and submarine attacks had prevented her from making any forays into the Atlantic so far. No. 617, together with No. 9 Squadron – whose Lancasters had also been modified to carry Tallboys – had already made two attempts to sink her; the first time, on 10 September, they had flown to the Russian airfield of Yagodnik, on the Archangel Peninsula, which was considerably closer than any British airfield to Kaa Fjord, where the battleship was then anchored.

Five days later, twenty-one Lancasters had set out from Yagodnik to attack the *Tirpitz* at a new anchorage in Alten Fjord; the weather over the target had been good, but the Germans laid a massive smokescreen over the fjord as the bombers approached, and by the time they reached their release-point the battleship was completely obscured. However, the bombardiers had taken the *Tirpitz*'s flak, which could be seen rising through the smoke in glowing streams, as their aiming-point, and some were confident that hits had been obtained.

In fact, one Tallboy had exploded on her bow, wrecking it almost completely from the stern to the forward gun turret. Her main engines were also damaged, and it was estimated that even if she could make her way to a fully equipped shipyard, it would be nine months at least before she could be made fully seaworthy again. The Germans therefore decided to move her to Tromsø, where her heavy armament might be used to help repel some future Allied landing.

The British Admiralty had no way of knowing that the *Tirpitz* no longer presented a threat to the convoys; she was still afloat, and so in their eyes she was still a menace. The two squadrons were once again briefed to attack her, and since Tromsø was two hundred miles closer to the British Isles than the battleship's previous anchorages, it was decided to mount the raid from Lossiemouth in Scotland.

On the morning of 29 October eighteen Lancasters of 617 Squadron, led by Wing Commander Tait, and eighteen of No. 9 under Wing Commander J. M. Bazin, took off in pouring rain and set course for Norway. The mission involved a round trip of 2,250 miles, so to compensate for the weight of the Tallboys and the extra fuel that had to be carried the Lancasters were stripped of every bit of equipment that was not considered absolutely necessary, including mid-upper gun turrets.

The bombers reached the target area at 9 a.m. and the crews had a clear view of their intended victim as they began their run-in. Then, at the very last moment, dense cloud drifted in from the sea and the swearing bombardiers were forced to drop their Tallboys through scanty gaps in the undercast.

Only one near miss was recorded. One Lancaster was damaged by flak and made a forced landing in Sweden; the rest all returned safely to base.

Bad weather delayed the third attempt for twelve days. Then, on 11 November, thirty Lancasters once more took off from Lossiemouth in the darkness before dawn, crossing the black crags of the Norwegian coast at sunrise and turned north towards their target.

The morning was brilliantly clear, and the battleship was clearly visible from a distance of twenty miles, her black silhouette resembling a spider nestling in the middle of a web of anti-submarine booms. This time the protective smokescreen came too late, and the Lancasters rode through waves of flak to drop their bombs. Wing Commander Tait's Tallboy was the first to go down, and as he turned away after release he saw bombs exploding all around the *Tirpitz*, obliterating her outline with rolling clouds of smoke and cascades of water. A moment later, a great plume of steam shot up through the darker clouds as a magazine exploded.

The *Tirpitz* was finished. As the Lancasters turned for home she capsized in the shallow waters of the fjord. More than a thousand members of her crew died, most of them trapped like rats inside her hull. Bomber Command's striking power had come a long way since those first puny attempts to destroy Germany's capital ships, back in the winter of 1939...

The destruction of the *Tirpitz* was perhaps the highlight of the Command's Tallboy operations, even though it was only a small part of the whole. Between June 1944 and the end of the European war, 854 of the six-ton bombs were dropped on targets in Germany and the Occupied Territories.

Tallboy, in fact, was a scaled-down version of an even larger bomb, a 22,000-lb monster known as 'Grand Slam' which was also designed by Barnes Wallis. Following the success of Tallboy, plans for the development of Grand Slam were pushed ahead and the first live bomb was dropped experimentally on the Ashley Walk bombing range in the New Forest on 13 March 1945. It blasted a crater thirty feet deep and 124 feet across.

Once again, No. 617 Squadron was chosen to pioneer the ten-ton bomb's operational debut. On 14 March one of the monsters was carried by a Lancaster flown by Squadron Leader C. C. Calder to the Bielefeld viaduct, near Bremen, with a form-ation of Tallboy-armed Lancasters following. Crews behind Calder noticed how his bomber's wings arced upwards at the tips in a graceful curve as they took the strain of the bomb's enormous weight. The weapon itself was recessed into the bomb bay, the bomb doors having been removed.

The Grand Slam speared into marshy ground thirty yards away from one of the viaduct's arches, producing a spurt of mud. It detonated a hundred feet below the surface, blasting a huge underground cavern into which five hundred feet of the viaduct collapsed. A shower of Tallboys completed the work of destruction.

Forty Grand Slams went down on German targets before the end of the war, all of them dropped by 617 Squadron. Bridges were the main objectives, but the ten-ton bombs were also aimed at U-boat pens in north Germany and heavy gun positions on Heligoland. One of the final missions was flown against Germany's last pocket battleship, the *Lützow*, on 13 April 1945, but although it had been originally planned to sink her with a Grand Slam it was in fact a Tallboy that ripped out her bottom.

With the war in Europe over, No. 617 Squadron began training for a new phase of operations, against the Japanese. As part of 'Tiger Force', the Bomber Command contingent that would join the Americans in the strategic air offensive against Japan, the squadron was to be based on the island of Okinawa, and drop its Tallboys and Grand Slams on the bridges that connected Kyushu to the main Japanese island of Honshu. The plan was for the Americans to storm ashore on Kyushu, so 617 Squadron would have played a vital part in preventing Japanese reinforcements flooding over to resist the invaders.

But the squadron never bombed Japan. Just when it was within a few weeks of leaving for the Far East, two bombs whose awesome power made Grand Slam seem like a firecracker brought the six-year holocaust of World War II to an end.